All Nations in God's Purpose

All Nations in God's Purpose

What the Bible teaches about missions

H. Cornell Goerner

Broadman Press
Nashville, Tennessee

Scripture portions marked (NIV) are from *The New International Version New Testament.* Copyright © 1973 by the New York Bible Society International. Used by permission of Zondervan Publishing House.

Those marked (RSV) are from the Revised Standard Version of the Bible, copyrighted 1946, 1952, © 1971, 1973.

Dewey Decimal Classification: 266.001
Subject heading: MISSIONS—BIBLICAL TEACHING

Library of Congress Catalog Card Number: 78-50360
Printed in the United States of America

DEDICATION

To missionaries overseas
and especially those who served
during my administration
in Africa, Europe, and the Near East.
They practice what I preach.
May their tribe increase!

Contents

Preface

This book was written for those who believe that the Bible is the inspired Word of God and who seek to understand better what God is saying to this generation. As one who spent more than twenty years on the faculty of a theological seminary, I am fairly well acquainted with the historical-critical method of Bible study, and I place a high evaluation upon solid scholarship in this field. I am aware of the documentary hypothesis, J, E, D, and P, Deutero- and Trito-Isaiah, Form Criticism, and other technical pursuits. I believe profoundly in the importance of getting at the meaning of the original Hebrew and Greek texts, as far as this is possible.

But I believe just as strongly that the Bible becomes the living Word for each individual when it is read devotionally, without undue concern for critical questions; and that it is not a book intended for experts only. Regardless of the historical background and the date and authorship of each separate book, the Bible has a message which is timeless and eternally contemporary. When it is read with an open mind and a sensitive heart, the Book speaks. And although each book within the Bible has its own message and the intensive study of a single book or chapter brings a reward, there is need from time to time to listen for the message of the Bible as a whole.

I have therefore tried to write for the serious Bible student with or without theological training, hoping that the average lay person in the church will find the book readable and that ministers also may consider it worthy of their attention. If seminary students should find it helpful and challenging, my satisfaction would be full.

Unless otherwise indicated, all Scripture quotations are from the *New American Standard Bible* (NASB). Copyright © The Lockman Foundation 1960, 1962, 1963, 1968, 1971, 1972, 1973, 1975. I am grateful for permission from the publishers to make these extensive quotations.

I have felt free at times to make my own translation from the Hebrew or Greek, or to paraphrase a biblical passage in order to bring out the meaning more clearly for modern readers. Such passages are identified in the footnotes.

In the first chapter I explain in some detail my indebtedness to Dr. W. O. Carver, my own seminary teacher of other years. I am grateful also to Dr. Helen Falls, professor of missions at New Orleans Baptist Theological Seminary, and to Dr. Lavell Seats, who holds a similar position at Midwestern Baptist Theological Seminary; both of them read much of the manuscript in its earlier stages and made valuable suggestions. John E. Mills, Paul W. Travis, my daughter, Cornelia Clipp, and her husband, Marvin, have also been helpful; and my wife, Ruth, is ever my most sympathetic but honest critic.

To Mrs. Rebecca Sisk, who typed the first draft from my rough copy, and to Mrs. Virginia Wilkins, who prepared the final manuscript, I am deeply indebted.

I ask my Lord's forgiveness if I have failed to express clearly what I believe he has laid upon my heart.

I.
The Theme of the Bible

"What is the Bible all about?" The wise old professor threw out that question at the opening session of a class in Christian missions. He paused expectantly, as though waiting for one of the seminary students to venture an answer. Then, with a quizzical expression on his face, he shifted to another question: "Is it *all* about anything?"

To the surprised and puzzled class he proceeded to explain the purpose of his two provocative questions. Does the Bible have one consistent theme which dominates the whole book? Or is it a mere collection of books by many authors dealing with many different subjects? What is the Bible about, all of it? What is the unifying theme of these sixty-six books written by some forty different authors over a period of about 1,500 years? Are we justified in binding them all together in one book called "The Bible"?

Dr. W. O. Carver used this approach again and again in his classes at the Southern Baptist Theological Seminary in Louisville, Kentucky. Master teacher that he was, he did not at once give an answer to his own question but expected the class to work out the answer in the weeks which followed. Through lectures, thoughtful questions directed to individual students, and open group discussion, the class moved through the Bible from Genesis to Revelation, tracing the theme of God's redemptive plan for all the peoples of the earth. No one who worked responsibly through that basic course with Dr. Carver could ever read his Bible in quite the same way as he had read it before entering the class.

For years Carver used as a textbook *Missions in the Plan of the Ages,* which he had written in 1909.[1] The title was from Paul's expression in Ephesians 3:11 "according to the eternal purpose which he purposed in Christ Jesus our Lord" (KJV). Carver used his own translation based on the Greek text "according to the Plan of the Ages." This plan, that the Gentiles should be fellow heirs of the Kingdom, along with the Jews; fellow members of the same body, the church; and fellow partakers of all the promises given to Abraham, Carver found summarized in Ephesians 3:6, but fully developed in the Bible as a whole. For him this term expressed "the theme of the Bible." Hundreds of pastors and missionaries who went from his classes to a ministry of service felt themselves to be an integral part of "the Plan of the Ages" and served the more devotedly because of this controlling idea.

Carver put the same thought into another catchy title: *All the World in All the Word.*[2] This small book was written at the request of Woman's Missionary Union of the Southern Baptist Convention, and for years was used as a study book by that organization. Years later in his autobiography, Carver wrote sadly:

This book was not written for the pastors. It was hoped that they would find it useful, but they took little interest in it. When they spoke of it, in the majority of cases, they got the title wrong, revealing that they had no real insight into the purpose or nature of my effort to show that the whole world enters definitely into every part of the word of God in the Bible. That remains one of my deep griefs about ministers, they have so little understanding of the major purpose of God and the universal outreach of his love dominating the entire Scriptures.[3]

"The major purpose of God and the universal outreach of his love"—this was what W. O. Carver regarded as the dominant theme of the entire Bible. His own life was dominated by the deep conviction that this was what the Bible was all about. And believing the Bible as he did, he was profoundly concerned that the message intended for all mankind should be spread abroad as widely as possible in his generation. This made him the missionary statesman that he was.

I first sat in W. O. Carver's class in September 1930. At once I was impressed with the profundity of his insight and the breadth of his scholarship. No one had ever opened up the Scriptures for me in this fashion before. Never had I grasped the consistent theme which runs through the Bible and binds it all together as one beautiful yet sobering whole. In 1932, as I began my graduate studies, Carver asked me to serve as Fellow for his undergraduate classes, and in that capacity I continued to audit the same courses on the biblical basis of missions for the next three years. His lectures, which I was privileged to hear repeatedly, revealed rich variety even as the same general subject matter was covered again and again. As a result, my thoughts became so enriched with his insights that it would now be impossible for me to determine which ideas are traceable directly to his influence and which may be due to my own originality or to some other forgotten source. I have repeatedly expressed my indebtedness to Carver and have aspired to transmit to others the inspiration I received from him.

Awed by Carver's grasp of the Scriptures, I found my-self seeking to analyze it. At first I theorized that it was due to the influence of the apostle Paul, whom he admired so much, and whose writings in the original Greek he had studied in depth. I still believe that W. O. Carver understood the mind of Paul as few scholars ever have. But then I came to see that it was not so much Paul as the Lord Jesus himself who had given my teacher the "key to the Scriptures." I began to look forward to one particular lecture which usually came about the middle of the school term. It was an imaginative meditation upon the first appearance of the risen Christ to the entire group of his disciples in the upper room on the evening of the resurrection day as recorded in Luke 24.

The story begins as two disillusioned disciples walk sadly from Jerusalem toward their home in the village of Emmaus. They had been convinced that Jesus of Nazareth was the long-awaited Messiah, and that he would somehow deliver the nation of Israel from its shameful bondage to the Roman Empire, and with God's help establish a kingdom even more glorious than that of David and Solomon. How this could be accomplished they did not know, but surely one who could heal the sick, feed multitudes miraculously, and even raise the dead to life must be Israel's best hope for national re-demption. They had had faith to believe that Jesus would lead their people to a new day. But now that hope had been shattered. Three days ago he had been arrested, given a hasty mock trial, condemned, crucified, and laid in a rocky tomb.

To be sure, some of the women claimed that they had seen a vision of angels that morning who declared that

Jesus was actually alive. But it was probably wishful thinking on the part of some neurotic women, for there was no doubt that Jesus was dead and buried.

As they talked of these things, a stranger joined them. Dusk was falling and they hardly looked up as they continued walking. Besides, the stranger seemed surprisingly uninformed. He appeared not even to know of the tragedy that had occurred in that miscarriage of justice.

But wait—was he uninformed, or did he know something they needed to know? The stranger began to quote Scripture from Moses and the Prophets indicating that the Messiah, when he came, would not make a mighty display of pomp and power, but rather would suffer vicariously for the people, and at last be killed and buried, to rise again in triumph on the third day.

Could this be so? The two wondered. They had read some of those Scriptures before, but never understood them as the stranger was now explaining them. Arriving at their village, they begged the unknown teacher to spend the night with them, hoping to receive further instruction. The stranger at first hesitated and then accepted the invitation.

Hastily the two prepared food for their unexpected guest. Assigning him the place of honor at their humble table, they invited him to bless the food. And then it happened! As he broke the bread and offered a prayer of thanksgiving they suddenly recognized him. (Perhaps they had seen him break bread before.) It was Jesus himself, alive in their presence! He had indeed suffered as he said the Messiah must, and had risen from the dead, according to the Scriptures!

No sooner did the light dawn upon their slow but now joyful hearts than Jesus disappeared from their sight.

Jubilant at their discovery, hunger forgotten, they rose from the table and hurried back to Jerusalem, some seven miles away, eager to share the good news with the other disciples. Straight to the accustomed meeting place they went, where they knew they would find the disciples in an upper room meeting secretly for fear of the Jewish leaders. They gave a secret knock and were admitted, only to find that Peter had broken the news. He too had seen the risen Lord and was excitedly seeking to convince the rest that the women had been right after all—Jesus *was* alive, and had appeared to Simon Peter!

As the two from Emmaus sought to add their testimony to that of Peter, and others in the group were trying to decide whether to believe them, they all suddenly became aware of another Presence! Jesus himself stood in their midst. Startled and fearful, the disciples thought they were seeing a ghost. But Jesus calmed their fears, saying, "Why are you so frightened, and why do you doubt what you are seeing? Look carefully at my hands and feet, and see that it is I myself. Touch me and prove it, for you know that a ghost does not have flesh and bones, as you see that I have" (Luke 24:38-39, author's paraphrase).

They still could hardly believe it! It was just too good to be true! They wondered how it could be. Seeing their doubt, Jesus asked, "Do you have anything here to eat?" They gave him a piece of broiled fish and he took it and ate it in their sight, demonstrating the reality of his resurrected body.

Jesus then said to the wondering group, "This is just what I kept telling you before my crucifixion: that all things which are written about me, the Messiah, in the Law of Moses, in the Prophets, and in the Psalms must be fulfilled." Then he opened their minds that they might be able to understand the scriptures which he had quoted to them before but which they now really understood for the first time (Luke 24:44-45, author's paraphrase).

"Then he opened their minds." I shall never forget how Dr. Carver made these words live for his students. "Most of us have closed minds," he would declare, "just as the disciples had. We think we know what the Bible teaches and are reluctant to admit an idea that may force us to rearrange our thinking. It is a wonderful thing when the Lord can get our minds open, and then get us to open the Bible and place the open Bible in our opened minds." Looking back, many of his students could see that this was exactly what Carver was trying to do: help the Holy Spirit open the minds of young ministers so that they would understand for the first time the profound truths of the Bible which he opened up to them.

Carver then made a point with which I fully agree. Verse 45 is a brief statement which covers a teaching session that must have lasted for two or three hours. It was the most memorable seminar ever conducted, as the risen Christ interpreted the messianic passages within the entire Old Testament to eleven apostles and other mystified disciples. Jesus reminded them that there were things written about him "in the Law of Moses, and the Prophets and the Psalms." To this day the Hebrew Bible is divided into three major sections: The Law, the Prophets, and the Writings. Central in the Writings are the Psalms, so this was a popular way of designating the section which also contained Daniel, Job, and certain other writings. The reference is therefore to the entire Old Testament, in the broadest sense. In each of the three sections there were scriptures referring to the promised Messiah.

Jesus had previously pointed out many of these passages. Beginning just after Peter's great confession, he had tried to prepare the disciples for his impending death. As Matthew 16:20-21 records:

Then He warned the disciples that they should tell no one that He was the Christ. From that time Jesus Christ began to show His disciples that He must go to Jerusalem, and suffer many things from the elders and chief priests and scribes, and be killed, and be raised up on the third day.

"He began to show them" from the Scriptures. He continued this instruction in a special session with Peter, James, and John just after his transfiguration, pointing out that "it was written" in the Scriptures that he must die (Mark 9:12). During that last week he had said it again:

"Behold, we are going up to Jerusalem, and all things which are written through the prophets about the Son of Man will be accomplished. For He will be delivered up to the Gentiles, and will be mocked and mistreated and spit upon, and after they have scourged Him, they will kill Him, and the third day He will rise again." And they understood none of these things, and this saying was hidden from them, and they did not comprehend the things that were said (Luke 18:31-34).

Now for the first time they were ready to understand what he had tried in vain to explain to them earlier. He probably quoted one verse after another. Or he may have called for some member of the group to turn to a passage in Moses, or in one of the prophets, or in a Psalm, and read it aloud from the parchment scroll, so that he could then lift out certain words and phrases and explain their full meaning. To quote and expound all the pertinent passages would have taken time; it must have been near midnight when the risen Lord finally closed the session by summarizing the essential teachings.

Between verses 45 and 46, one must visualize the two-hour seminar with detailed commentary on many specific scriptures. Verse 46 is the condensed summary, introduced by the words, "Thus it is written." The meaning is, "Here then is what stands written." The messianic teachings which Jesus said must be fulfilled are then stated under two concise points: (1) that the Messiah must suffer and be raised from the dead the third day; and (2) that repentance for forgiveness of sins should be proclaimed in his name to all nations, beginning from Jerusalem.

There can be little doubt about some of the passages Jesus quoted to support the first point. Surely Isaiah 53 and Psalm 22 were carefully expounded, and the disciples readily understood that the sufferings described there had been fulfilled on Calvary's cross three days earlier (Luke 22:37; Matt. 27:35, 46). He probably quoted again Zechariah 13:7 as he had just after the Last Supper (Matt. 26:31). He may have referred again to Jonah's three days and nights in the belly of the sea monster as symbolic of his own three days and nights in the tomb (Matt. 12:40). Other passages could have been cited concerning the Messiah's death and resurrection, and much attention has been given to the theological necessity of his death.

But Jesus did not end his discourse there. He went on to explain the reason for his suffering and the extent of its effectiveness. This too he found in the Scriptures and explained to his disciples during that first appearance to the entire group. His death had been in order to make possible the forgiveness of sins for those who repent and accept him; this was not limited to Israel, but was to be proclaimed *to all the nations.*

Jesus had found his Father's plan for world redemption

revealed throughout the Hebrew Bible. In all three sections, the Law of Moses, the Prophets, and the Psalms, he found it written, that on the basis of his death and resurrection, repentance for the forgiveness of sin was to be proclaimed to all the nations, Gentiles as well as Jews. His disciples were to begin witnessing in Jerusalem, and then to expand their witness throughout Judea, up into Samaria, and on out to the distant parts of the earth to *all nations!*

If Luke's account is authentic, as Carver believed it to be and as I am deeply convinced, then Jesus intended from the beginning of his ministry to project a worldwide mission. He consciously and deliberately gave his life as a ransom for many (Matt. 20:28), Jews and Gentiles alike, and became the propitiation for the sins of the whole world (1 John 2:2). The universality of his mission was not only implicit; it was explicit and purposefully planned.

Jesus had found "all the world in all the Word." He found God's redemptive purpose for all peoples revealed in the Scriptures. His life and his death were the direct expression of what he had found written concerning the world mission of the Messiah.

In a book published in 1944, I tried to trace some of the Scriptures to which Jesus may have referred during that memorable messianic seminar, and at other times in his ministry.[4] The title reflected the theme of the book *Thus It Is Written,* obviously based upon words of Jesus in Luke 24:46-47, with the emphasis upon *all the nations.* The book was rather widely used, and has been translated into seven foreign languages, but is now out of print in English. Convinced of the need for a deeper understanding of the universal purpose of God and a rediscovery of "the Plan of the Ages," I resolved to offer another book to the Christian public. It is a guide to the study of the Bible itself and really should be read with an open Bible in hand.

No effort is made to prove that Jesus used all the Scriptures cited, but the hope is that we may read our Bible as Jesus read his, letting God speak concerning his purpose for the world and for us, even if it calls for suffering and sacrifice on our part. In particular, we shall be emphasizing passages which express God's concern for *all peoples*, and his plan to take from among *all nations* a people redeemed and blessed according to his eternal purpose.

In the next three chapters we seek to understand how Jesus found God's purpose for all nations in the books of Moses, in the writings of the Prophets, and in the Psalms. We shall then review the fulfillment of these Scriptures in the ministry of Jesus and his world outreach through chosen witnesses.

For that *is* what the Bible is all about!

Notes

[1] First published by Fleming H. Revell Company, *Missions in the Plan of the Ages* went through three editions before going out of print. It was republished in 1951 by Broadman Press, Nashville, Tennessee, and continues to be used, although it is now again out of print.

[2] Published by Baptist Sunday School Board, Nashville, Tennessee. Now out of print.

[3] *Out of His Treasure.* Unfinished memoirs of W. O. Carver. Nashville: Broadman Press, 1956), pp. 112-13.

[4] Henry Cornell Goerner, *Thus It Is Written: The Missionary Motif in the Scriptures,* (Nashville: Broadman Press, 1944).

II.
All Nations in the Books of Moses

God's concern for all his peoples is clearly revealed in the Pentateuch, the first five books of the Bible, commonly attributed to Moses. Stated repeatedly in Genesis, "the Book of Beginnings," the universal purpose is reaffirmed again and again in other Mosaic books, as it shines through the mass of legal and ceremonial details which threaten to obscure the central theme of the Scriptures.

The first eleven chapters of Genesis are sweepingly universal. The story of mankind from the creation to the call of Abraham is sketched in bold strokes: One God created one world and one human family. One common problem promptly infected the whole race: the sin problem. For ages, God dealt with the rebellious human race as a whole, at one point destroying all mankind except Noah and his family. The descendants of Noah, all kinsmen, made a new beginning, but soon the sin problem was as grievous as before. God decided to use a new method, dealing with one man and his family, in a slow, painful, educational, and redemptive process, aimed ultimately at winning his rebellious creatures back to himself in willing obedience.

So at Genesis 12 the story narrows down to Abraham and his descendants. Thereafter, the Hebrew race is in the focus of the biblical perspective, and other races seem to be on the fringes or out of sight altogether. But the Bible makes perfectly clear that this is because God has a special purpose to be achieved through Abraham and his descendants and that ultimately all the other races, tribes, and peoples share fully in that purpose. This is first stated at the time of the call of Abraham, in Genesis 12:1-3:

Now the LORD said to Abram,
"Go forth from your country,   And from your relatives And from your father's house,   To the land which I will show you;   And I will make you a great nation,   And I will bless you,   And make your name great;   And so you shall be a blessing;   And I will bless those who bless you,   And the one who curses you I will curse.   And in you all the families of the earth shall be blessed."

The key words are, "In you *all the families of the earth* shall be blessed."

Much has been said about God's promises to Abraham, and very little about the command or commission to Abraham: "You shall be a blessing." Here the Hebrew word may be either a future tense or the imperative: the form would be the same. Either translation, "thou shalt be a blessing," or, "be thou a blessing"—as a command—is equally accurate. When God declares it is to be, this should be taken as a command. The meaning is clear: "Abraham, I am going to bless you, and you in turn are to bless others, allowing each blessing I give you to pass through you to others, in ever-widening circles, until at last all the families of the earth will be blessed, just as you have been blessed."

The word *families* does not refer to the simple family unit, composed of a man, his wife, and their children. Rather, it denotes extended families or ethnic groups, and could well be translated, "all the tribes (or nations) of the earth."

Some new translations, such as the Revised Standard Version, render Genesis 12:3, "and by you all the families of the earth shall bless themselves." But the Hebrew verb here is passive (Niphal) and should be translated, "shall be blessed," as in the marginal reading of the RSV.[1] *Today's English Version* reads, "And through you I will bless all the nations," properly emphasizing that it is God who will bless, using Abraham and his descendants as instruments for his purpose.

God did indeed choose Abraham for a special purpose, and promised to bless him and his descendants. But from the beginning it was made plain that this did not mean that the sons of Abraham were to be God's pampered pets, receiving favors denied to others. Rather, they were to be God's channel of blessing, allowing every blessing received to flow through them to others, until all the nations of the earth should be blessed just as Abraham's descendants were first blessed.

This principle of divine election for universal service is stated, not once, but five times in the book of Genesis. In words quite similar, but varying just enough to bring out the meaning with rich variety, God's purpose to bless all the nations is repeated twice to Abraham, and then to his son, Isaac, and his grandson, Jacob. Like the recurring refrain of a beautiful song, the words constitute the theme of Genesis, and thus the controlling idea of the entire Bible. Each statement was made at a time of crisis when there was need for a reaffirmation of God's purpose for all his peoples.

Genesis 18:17-19 represents God talking to himself just before the destruction of Sodom and Gomorrah:

And the LORD said, "Shall I hide from Abraham what I am about to do, since Abraham will surely become a great and mighty nation, and in him all the nations of the earth shall be blessed? For I have chosen him, in order that he may command his children and his household after him to keep the way of the LORD by doing righteousness and justice; in order that the LORD may bring upon Abraham what He has spoken about him."

The greatest blessing that any man can receive is a knowledge of the nature and purpose of God. Here Abraham was about to receive his first dramatic lesson: God is a God of righteousness, who will not allow wickedness to go unpunished. He is patient and merciful, but there is a point beyond which his patience will not go. Judgment is certain. Sin must be punished and excessive wickedness wiped out. Righteousness must be established. If there had been even ten righteous men in Sodom and Gomorrah, the cities would have been spared. But wickedness was so rampant that all had to be destroyed in righteous judgment.

We may reverently paraphrase God's soliloquy: "Shall I keep from Abraham what I am about to do? No, of course not. I must tell him in advance that I am going to destroy these wicked cities, because of their sinfulness and my righteousness. Then when it happens, Abraham will know why it happened. He will know that it was no freak of nature, but my righteous act, and will understand that this is the way I will always deal with wickedness. He will tell his children, and they can tell their children, and their children's children, and others also, passing on the truth that the God of the universe is a God of righteousness, who will not allow sin to go unpunished. They will then govern their lives accordingly and avoid judgment. As this revelation of my nature is passed on from generation to generation, and from family to family, all the nations of the earth will be blessed as they recognize my righteousness and save themselves from judgment and destruction such as came upon the citizens of Sodom and Gomorrah."

This has been God's intention from the time of Abraham. Unfortunately, there are still families, tribes, and nations, to say nothing of countless individuals, who have not yet received this first blessing intended for them. They do not know that they are dealing with the God of righteousness, who will judge and punish wickedness. The blessing of Abraham needs to be shared with them before it is too late.

For the third time the all-inclusive purpose of God was revealed to Abraham after he obeyed God and proved his willingness to offer his son Isaac as a sacrifice on Mount Moriah, as recorded in Genesis 22:16-18:

"By Myself I have sworn," declares the LORD, "because you have done this thing, and have not withheld your son, your only son, indeed I will greatly bless you, and I will greatly multiply your seed as the stars of the heavens, and as the sand which is on the seashore; and your seed shall possess the gate of their enemies. And in your seed all the nations of the earth shall be blessed, because you have obeyed My voice."

The blessing involved in this experience was two-fold. First it was revealed that God requires full surrender and complete obedience to his will. Sometimes this must be blind obedience and unquestioning faith. Abraham could not see how God could fulfill his promise if he sacrificed his only son. Yet, if God required this, Abraham was willing to obey, and for this he was blessed.

The second part of the blessing is not always clearly

perceived. It was revealed, for the first time, that God does not require human sacrifice. He honored Abraham's willingness to sacrifice his son, but stopped his upraised hand with the command, "Do not slay the lad." The lesson was clear. God demands absolute obedience, but takes no pleasure in human sacrifice. An animal may be substituted. The principle of substitutionary sacrifice here established remained in effect throughout the Old Testament era, and came to glorious fulfillment when Jesus came as "the Lamb of God who takes away the sin of the world" (John 1:29). God revealed to Abraham at Mount Moriah that it is the intention of the heart, and not the substance of the sacrifice, that makes a worshiper acceptable to God.

This double blessing was to be passed on to Abraham's descendants and through them to others, until "all the nations of the earth shall be blessed." As they learn obedience, the blessing will come. But obedience does not involve human sacrifice. Never after that time did the Hebrews offer human sacrifice, although the Canaanite tribes surrounding them continued that revolting practice for many generations. Even today in some parts of the world human sacrifice is performed because there are tribes that have not yet received the blessing of Abraham which was supposed to be passed on to them: namely, that God does require complete obedience but does not accept human sacrifice.

The fourth statement of God's universal purpose is found in Genesis 26:2-5, this time addressed to Isaac:

And the LORD appeared to him and said, "Do not go down to Egypt; stay in the land of which I shall tell you. Sojourn in this land and I will be with you and bless you, for to you and to your descendants I will give all these lands, and I will establish the oath which I swore to your father Abraham. And I will multiply your descendants as the stars of heaven, and will give your descendants all these lands; and by your descendants all the nations of the earth shall be blessed."

The situation was not quite so dramatic as with Abraham. Isaac was a quiet man, not a colorful character such as his father Abraham or his son Jacob. He was inclined toward obedience, but at this point was tempted to go down to Egypt, because of the famine in his land. He needed reassurance that God would care for him, even as he had cared for Abraham. This came in the one profound spiritual encounter recorded for Isaac. He was told that he could trust God to provide for his needs, since God had a purpose which went far beyond Isaac's own importance. Through him and his descendants *all the nations of the earth* were destined to be blessed. This was the purpose of God! It would surely be accomplished!

More dramatic was the experience of Jacob. Crafty as he was, he had bought the birthright of his older brother, Esau, and then secured the paternal blessing from Isaac by deceit. Fearful of revenge from Esau, he fled from his home and spent his first lonely night at Bethel, where God appeared to him in a dream, with words of assurance and promise found in Genesis 28:13-15:

"I am the LORD, the God of your father Abraham and the God of Isaac; the land of which you lie, I will give it to you and to your descendants. Your descendants shall also be like the dust of the earth, and you shall spread out to the west and to the east and to the north and to the south; *and in you and in your descendants shall all the families of the earth be blessed.* And behold, I am with you, and will keep you wherever you go, and will bring you back to this land; for I will not leave you until I have done what I have promised you" (author's italics).

Jacob's encounter was a further self-revelation of God. It brought out the fact that Yahweh was not confined to a certain locality, as Jacob had been inclined to believe, but was everywhere present. Surrounded by people who worshiped foreign deities, Jacob may have feared that he was in "heathen territory" when he got beyond the realm controlled by his father, Isaac, the only true worshiper of Yahweh known to Jacob. But Yahweh spoke to him, identified himself by name,[2] and declared, "I am with you and will keep you wherever you go." There is no area beyond God's reach; he is omnipresent. This was clearly revealed for the first time to Jacob. Upon awaking, his first words were, "Surely [Yahweh] is in this place, and I did not know it" (v. 16). Never after that did he doubt God's presence; and he told his children that Yahweh was everywhere and would care for them since he had a purpose that through them all the tribes of the earth should be blessed.

It is difficult to understand how the Jews could have overlooked or virtually ignored these statements, which literally dominate the book of Genesis and give the reason for their existence as a nation and their preservation as a Chosen People. The prophets sought to keep alive the sense of God's purpose for them and their mission to the nations, but across the years their struggle for power and the influence of worldly ambition caused them to claim God's promise to make them a great nation and give them a land in which to live, while they seemed to forget the basic purpose of it all: *"Through you and your descendants all the nations of the earth shall be blessed."*

But Jesus knew his Bible, and it is obvious that these passages in Moses were essential in his thinking and his plans for his own ministry. There is no record that he ever quoted these words directly, but they were fresh in the mind of Simon Peter when he and John went to the Temple shortly after Pentecost and created a sensation by healing a man who had been lame from his birth. To the curious crowd that gathered, Peter preached Christ as the Holy and Righteous One, the Messiah who had suffered in fulfillment of the Scriptures, and called for repentance in his name. He quoted two passages from Moses, Deuteronomy 18:15, to which we shall turn shortly, and Genesis 22:18: "And in your seed all the families of the earth shall be blessed."

Why did Peter use these passages? Probably because Jesus had used them a few days earlier as he explained the meaning of his death and resurrection (Luke 24:44-49). It is instructive to notice how close Peter came on that occasion to declaring that the message of repentance was intended for all and must be declared to all the nations. Addressing a Jewish audience, with all the prejudice against Gentiles that Peter understood so well, he could not bring himself to proclaim it fully, but strongly implied it in these words: "When God raised up his servant, he sent him first to you to bless you by turning each one of you from his wicked ways" (Acts 3:26, NIV).

"God sent him to you Jews *first*," said Peter. Who then was to be second and third? The obvious implication is the families of the earth who have just been mentioned as destined to receive a blessing through the sons of the covenant. Peter almost said it: "You Jews are the first to be blessed by learning of God's Suffering Servant, who was foretold by the prophets. But after you, all the Gentiles are to be blessed, and you are to be the means of blessing them, as you share with them what you have learned concerning the Messiah. Thus you will fulfill what God promised to Abraham." Peter would not have quoted these words from Moses if the risen Christ had not quoted them in his hearing and burned them into his memory. The occasion did not demand that he make the full application forecast by Christ: "that repentance for forgiveness of sins should be proclaimed in His name to all the nations," but he was faithful in "beginning from Jerusalem" (Luke 24:47) and announcing the message "to the Jews first," fully aware that others were somehow to receive the same blessing later.

The Book of Exodus

The second book of Moses, Exodus, describes how the Hebrew people, once a motley multitude of ex-slaves, became a nation, with a "constitution" and a clear reason for being. The "constitution" is the God-given Ten Commandments recorded in Exodus 20, with all the additional legislation set forth in the remainder of the Mosaic books. More important for our purpose is what might be called "the preamble to the constitution," recorded in Exodus 19. This states the *reason* for God's choice of one people from among all the peoples of the earth, the *condition* under which any people may continue to serve as God's special people, and the *function* which they are expected to perform. All of this is contained in four strategic verses, Exodus 19:3-6, which is the entire communication from God to Moses during their first encounter on Mt. Sinai. The Ten Commandments were not given at that time. No final commitment of any kind was made. God's plan was explained to Moses, and he was told to explain it to all the people. They were to be given the choice, either to agree to the conditions and become God's special people, or to decline the honor and refuse the responsibility. It must be a voluntary decision on the part of the people as a whole. Moses could not decide for them, but was to present the proposal, get their decision, and report back to God. Note carefully this significant statement:

And Moses went up to God, and the LORD called to him from the mountain, saying, "Thus you shall say to the house of Jacob and tell the sons of Israel: 'You yourselves have seen what I did to the Egyptians, and how I bore you on eagles' wings, and brought you to Myself. Now then, if you will indeed obey My voice and keep My covenant, then you shall be My own possession among all the peoples, for all the earth is Mine; and you shall be to Me a kingdom of priests and a holy nation.' These are the words that you shall speak to the sons of Israel."

Notice God's affirmation of his ownership of all peoples: "You shall be My own possession [my special treasure] among all the peoples, *for all the earth is Mine*" (author's italics). The Hebrew word, *segullah,* denoted the personal, individual treasures of a king, who owned everything in his kingdom in an official way, but had certain things that were cherished privately. God was not here relinquishing his claim upon any of his peoples. They all belonged to him, and he was concerned for them all. But he needed a special kind of people for a particular purpose.

Note next the condition stated: *"If* you will indeed obey My voice and keep My covenant." The alternative is clearly implied: "If you do not obey, if you break the covenant, then you shall no longer be my people. I cannot use you if you are not obedient. The choice is yours. Will you agree to my terms? Will you consent to be bound by my covenant? If so, I will make you a kingdom of priests, a holy nation. That is what I need to deal with the other nations of the earth. Will you agree to become my holy priest-nation?"

The function of a priest is well-known. He serves as a mediator between God and the congregation he serves. He makes the will of God known to the people and makes the people acceptable to God. But the picture here is not of an individual priest ministering to a group of individual persons. What God wants is a kingdom of priests, a priest-kingdom, a nation composed entirely of priests, ministering to the other nations and peoples, who form, as it were, the congregation. The holy priest-nation is to mediate between God and the other nations, making God's will known to the nations (the Gentiles), and making the nations acceptable to God, as they respond to the revelation of his righteous character and his will for all peoples. The Chosen People must be holy, set apart for God's service, and they must minister to the other peoples, sharing with them all that God reveals, and thus becoming a channel of blessing.

How fully this was understood by the Hebrew people we cannot know. We can read back into these inspired words of Scripture more than is said explicitly; but it all lies implicit in this passage in which we can see the purpose of God revealed. Later warnings from Moses make it clear that the people did understand at least to some degree, and that they were responsible for the decision they made and were to be judged according to their obedience under the covenant. There is abundant evidence that Jesus understood all that was involved, and that he came as the final messenger of judgment to a nation which had disobeyed God, had failed to serve as a priest-nation ministering to the Gentile nations in saving and redemptive ways, and was to be replaced by a new Chosen People, bound under a new covenant, to be sealed in his own blood, as the Lamb of God.

It should be noticed finally that Moses went down from the mountain, presented the divine proposal to the people, and in some form of democratic referendum they expressed their approval:

And all the people answered together and said, "All that the LORD has spoken we will do!" And Moses brought back the words of the people to the LORD (Ex. 19:8).

Then and only then were preparations made for giving the Ten Commandments. The preamble had been approved; there was now need for a constitution for the new nation. But the preamble stands as more significant than the constitution itself. And Jesus understood fully the awesome significance of the covenant relation and the ultimate result of disobedience.

There is no record that Jesus quoted Exodus 19:3-6, but Peter did, and we may assume that his understanding of this Scripture came directly from his Lord, who expounded it on that resurrection evening, just after the new covenant had been sealed with the remnant that was to be the nucleus of the new Israel, the new Chosen People. In a letter addressed not to Jews as such, but to "those who are chosen," both Jew and Gentile, scattered throughout Pontus, Galatia, Cappadocia, Asia, and Bithynia, Peter wrote:

But you are A CHOSEN RACE, A ROYAL PRIESTHOOD, A HOLY NATION, A PEOPLE FOR *God's* OWN POSSESSION, that you may proclaim the excellencies of Him who has called you out of darkness into His marvelous light; for you once were NOT A PEOPLE, but now you are THE PEOPLE OF GOD; you had not RECEIVED MERCY, but you have received mercy (I Pet. 2:9-10).[3]

The words of Moses in Exodus were in process of being fulfilled!

Leviticus, Numbers, Deuteronomy

Space will not permit detailed reference to other passages in the books of Moses which teach of God's concern for all peoples. Leviticus is heavy with legalistic regulations and ceremonial requirements which applied specifically to the Hebrews, but reminders of God's ownership of and concern for the Gentiles shine through at Leviticus 19:18,34. On more than one occasion Jesus quoted the eighteenth verse, and he exalted the commandment to love one's neighbor as oneself above all except the command to love God supremely (Mark 12:29-31; Matt. 19:19). It was possible to interpret the term "neighbor" as applying only to one's Jewish neighbor, and not to those of other races. This many scribes and rabbis did, as the lawyer who questioned Jesus on this point well knew. But verse 34 specifically commands that any alien residing among the Hebrews should be treated as a native, without any distinction, and that he also should be loved as one loves himself. Jesus underscored this wider interpretation in the parable of the good Samaritan, which was deliberately designed to contradict the racial prejudice among the Jews of that day (Luke 10:30-37). Moses could be cited as his authority, if any were needed.

Numbers 14 reinforces the conditional nature of the choice of the Hebrews as God's instrument for blessing all the other nations, making clear that God meant it when he said, "If you obey, then you shall be my special people, but if not . . . ." Earlier, after the people had made a golden calf and worshiped it, God threatened to destroy them and, beginning all over again, make of

Moses a great nation. Only the urgent intercessory prayer of Moses averted this calamity (Ex. 32:9-14). Now, some months later, after the report of the spies sent into the Promised Land, the people turned against Moses and Aaron, and proposed to choose new leaders and return to Egypt. They were on the point of stoning Moses when God intervened in a miraculous way. Note well his stern words in Numbers 14:11-12:

And the LORD said to Moses, "How long will this people spurn me? And how long will they not believe in Me, despite all the signs which I have performed in their midst? I will smite them with pestilence and dispossess them, and I will make you into a nation greater and mightier than they."

Again it was the earnest intercessory prayer of Moses that saved the people from destruction. God forgave them and gave them another chance, but not without severe punishment. All those who had rebelled were sentenced to wander in the wilderness until they died. Only Caleb and Joshua were spared to enter into the Promised Land, along with the younger generation who had not been responsible for the rebellion. Forty years of wandering may have seemed a heavy penalty for disobedience and lack of faith. But God explained why this punishment was necessary. So much was at stake! He was counting on this special people to be the means of spreading his glory throughout the whole earth as his kingdom of priests, his holy nation. So he declared to Moses with a solemn oath:

"I have pardoned, according to your word; but truly, as I live, and as all the earth shall be filled with the glory of the LORD, none of the men who have seen my glory and my signs which I wrought in Egypt and in the wilderness, and yet have put me to the proof these ten times and have not harkened to my voice, shall see the land which I swore to give to their fathers; and none of those who despised me shall see it,"(Num. 14:20-23, RSV).

Deuteronomy records the last words of Moses at the end of the wilderness wanderings, just before they began the conquest of the Promised Land. Moses reviews the events of those years, reminds them of their disobedience, and repeatedly warns them that in the future, if they disobey and break the covenant, God will withdraw his protection and allow them to be destroyed. Particularly strong are the warnings in Deuteronomy 4:23-26; 8:19-20; 28:15-45; 29:22-28; and 30:15-20.

In Deuteronomy 10:14-19, Moses reaffirms God's ownership of all the nations and marvels at his choice of Israel from among all the peoples. He reminds them that God does not show partiality, cannot be bribed, and has special concern for orphans, widows, and foreigners. He admonishes the Hebrews: "So show your love for the alien, for you were aliens in the land of Egypt" (v. 19).

Jesus answered every temptation in the wilderness with a quotation from Deuteronomy, giving evidence of his keen familiarity with the book. While there is no record that he ever quoted Deuteronomy 18:15-19, it is almost certain that he regarded himself as the one who fulfilled this prediction of a prophet like Moses whom God would raise up, whom the people were commanded to obey. Again, Peter gives the evidence that Jesus so interpreted this passage to his disciples. In the Temple soon after Pentecost, he quoted words which Jesus had probably put on his lips a few days earlier in the upper room:

Moses said, "THE LORD GOD SHALL RAISE UP FOR YOU A PROPHET LIKE ME FROM YOUR BRETHREN; TO HIM YOU SHALL GIVE HEED IN EVERYTHING HE SAYS TO

YOU. AND IT SHALL BE THAT EVERY SOUL THAT DOES NOT HEED THAT PROPHET SHALL BE UTTERLY DESTROYED FROM AMONG THE PEOPLE" (Acts 3:22-23).

Earlier, in answer to the attacks of Jewish leaders, Jesus had said:

"Do not think that I will accuse you before the Father; the one who accuses you is Moses, in whom you have set your hope. For if you believed Moses, you would believe Me; for he wrote of Me. But if you do not believe his writings, how will you believe My words?" (John 5:45-47).

Indeed, Moses wrote of the Messiah, and of his mission to all the nations, in fulfillment of the divine purpose that all the families of the earth shall be blessed through the descendants of Abraham, and that all the earth shall be filled with the glory of the Lord. Thus it is written, and thus it shall be!

Notes

[1] At Genesis 22:18 and 26:4 the reflexive verb (Hithpael) is used, and may be translated, "shall bless themselves," or, as *Today's English Version* has it, "will ask me to bless them as I have blessed your descendants." But here also, the Hebrew verb may have the force of a passive, and it is so translated in the Greek Septuagint, the King James Version, and the *New American Standard Bible.* This is consistent with New Testament quotations in Acts 3:25 and Galatians 3:8.

[2] It should be noted that whenever "the LORD" is printed in capitals, as here and in many other places, it translates the Hebrew word YAHWEH, the personal name, rather than *Elohim,* the general name of God, or *adonai,* the word for Lord, which is printed in lower case letters. This usage is observed in the King James Version, the Revised Standard Version, and the *New American Standard Bible.*

[3] See also 1 Peter 1:1. To the words of Exodus 19, Peter adds references to Hosea 1 and 2.

III.
All Nations in the Prophets

When Jesus declared that it was written in the Prophets that the Messiah must suffer, Isaiah 53 must have been central in his thinking. He knew that he was the Suffering Servant of the Lord. He was the "man of sorrows, and acquainted with grief" (v. 3). He was to be wounded for the transgressions and bruised for the iniquities of the people. The Lord was to lay upon him the iniquities of all those who had gone astray and turned every one to his own way. He would be brought as a lamb to the slaughter, and as a sheep before the shearers he would stand silent in the presence of his accusers. He knew that he would be "buried among the wicked," despite the fact that he had "done no violence," and there was "no deceit in his mouth." He must do God's will, but he would triumph in the end, as Isaiah foresaw:

Yet it pleased the LORD to bruise him; he hath put him to grief; when thou shall make his soul an offering for sin, he shall see his seed, he shall prolong his days, and the pleasure of the LORD shall prosper in his hand.
He shall see of the travail of his soul, and shall be satisfied; by his knowledge shall my righteous servant justify many; for he shall bear their iniquities.
Therefore will I divide him a portion with the great, and he shall divide the spoil with the strong; because he hath poured out his soul unto death: and he was numbered with the trans-

gressors; and he bare the sin of many, and made intercession for the transgressors (Isa. 53:10–12, KJV).

Eleven of the twelve verses in Isaiah 53 are quoted in the New Testament, all identifying Jesus as the Suffering Servant.[1] All four Gospels quote some portion of the chapter. When Philip was asked by the Ethiopian eunuch of whom the prophet spoke, he began at that same scripture and preached Jesus to him, ready to explain what Jesus had recently interpreted to his disciples (Acts 8:34).

This passage in Isaiah teaches not only the necessity of suffering, but also the assurance of ultimate triumph and the inauguration of a glorious new era worldwide in its significance. Remembering that the chapter divisions had not been designated in the Bible used by Jesus, it is instructive to take note of some verses just before and just after this crucial chapter. The sufferings of the Servant are set in the context of certain victory and the exaltation of the true God among all the nations of earth.

Isaiah 52:10 tells what God is about to do:

The Lord has bared His holy arm   In the sight of all the nations;   That all the ends of the earth may see   The salvation of our God.

Paradoxically, of the same one who is to suffer it is said: "Behold, My servant will prosper,   He will be high and lifted up, and greatly exalted" (Isa. 52:13). At verse 15 the text is uncertain, but the translation of the Revised Standard Version is probably correct: "so shall he startle many nations; kings shall shut their mouths because of him; for that which has not been told them they shall see, and that which they have not heard they shall understand." In other words, the highest authorities of the

Gentile nations will stand in awe and wonder, speechless at what is made known to them through the Suffering Servant. These verses are continuous with the chapter 53, and it is unfortunate that the chapter heading is inserted at this point.

Immediately after the sufferings described in Isaiah 53 comes a shout of rejoicing and the challenge to a world-wide mission. Again, it is unfortunate that the heading, "Isaiah 54," breaks the continuity of the narrative in our Bible. It was not in the Hebrew Bible used by Jesus, and there is no reason to believe that he stopped reading at the end of chapter 53. For as a result of the vicarious suffering endured by the Servant, a wonderful thing becomes possible. The people of God are now called upon to fulfill their mission to the Gentile nations. Like a barren woman who has no children but is about to give birth to many sons, Israel is called upon to build a bigger tabernacle, or tent of dwelling, to make room for all the new additions to the family:

Enlarge the place of your tent;   Stretch out the curtains of your dwellings, spare not; Lengthen your cords, And strengthen your pegs.   For you will spread abroad to the right and to the left.   And your descendants will possess nations, And they will resettle the desolate cities (Isa. 54:2–3).[2]

At Isaiah 55:3–5 there is a remarkable statement. God promised to make "an everlasting covenant" with his people, probably referring originally to the remnant spared after the Babylonian captivity. But to Jesus and the disciples to whom he may have interpreted these words, it would apply to the new Israel, who would be a witness to the peoples, and would call a nation they did not formerly know. "And a nation which knows you not will run to you, because of the Lord your God, even the Holy One of Israel" (v. 5).

As Jesus cleansed the Temple in Jerusalem, he quoted from Isaiah 56:7: "MY HOUSE SHALL BE CALLED A HOUSE OF PRAYER FOR ALL THE NATIONS" (Mark 11:17). The verse immediately preceding tells of a time when foreigners will join themselves to the Lord to minister to him and become his servants. Jesus fully understood that, after he had suffered, according to Isaiah 53, it was God's plan that repentance and forgiveness of sin should be proclaimed in his name to all the nations, according to Isaiah 54; 55; 56.

As a text for his first sermon at Nazareth, Jesus quoted Isaiah 61:1-2, declaring, "Today this Scripture has been fulfilled in your hearing" (Luke 4:21). This is in the context of that same sweeping passage concerning God's purpose for all the nations. At Isaiah 60:3 the prophet declares, "And nations will come to your light, And kings to the brightness of your rising." Isaiah 61:8-9 promises, "And I will make an everlasting covenant with them. Then their offspring will be known among the nations, and their descendants in the midst of the peoples." The urgency of making God's righteousness known among the Gentiles is expounded in Isaiah 62:1-2:

> For Zion's sake I will not keep silent,
> And for Jerusalem's sake I will not keep quiet,
> Until her righteousness goes forth like brightness,
> And her salvation like a torch that is burning.
> And the nations will see your righteousness,
> And all kings your glory;
> And you will be called by a new name,
> Which the mouth of the Lord will designate.

That Jesus had read the book of Isaiah to the end is clear from Mark 9:48, in which he quoted the very last verse, Isaiah 66:24, referring to Gehenna as a place "where their worm does not die, and the fire is not quenched." This indicates that he was also familiar with the passage immediately preceding those words, one of the most remarkable missionary messages in the entire Bible. Those who escape at the sign of judgment set in their midst are sent out to distant lands to proclaim God's glory. (Tarshish was Spain, in the far west. Javan was probably Greece. Other faraway places are listed, along with distant islands.) From all these places converts (brothers) will be brought to the house of the Lord, and he will make some of them priests and Levites (worship leaders). In the end, "all mankind" will acknowledge the one true God. Those who resist are brought to everlasting judgment. It is easy to visualize Jesus interpreting this wonderful passage to his disciples in the upper room and identifying the sign of judgment among the nations as the sign of the cross:

"For I know their works and their thoughts; the time is coming to gather all nations and tongues. And they shall come and see My glory.

"And I will set a sign among them and will send survivors from them to the nations: Tarshish, Put, Lud, Meshech, Rosh, Tubal, and Javan, to the distant coastlands that have neither heard My fame nor seen My glory. And they will declare My glory among the nations.

"Then they shall bring all your brethren from all the nations as a grain offering to the LORD, on horses, in chariots, in litters, on mules, and on camels, to My holy mountain Jerusalem," says the LORD, "just as the sons of Israel bring their grain offering in a clean vessel to the house of the LORD.

"I will also take some of them for priests and for Levites," says the LORD.

"For just as the new heavens and the new earth Which I will make will endure before Me," declares the LORD, "So your offspring and your name will endure. And it shall be from new moon to new moon and from sabbath to sabbath, all mankind will come to bow down before Me," says the LORD (Isa. 66:18-23).

The "Servant passages" which Jesus knew he was to fulfill actually begin at Isaiah 41:8. Although the term "Servant" had been originally applied to the nation of Israel, by the time of Jesus it was clear that the nation had failed to fulfill God's expectation and that even the remnant was unworthy to accomplish what the prophet had foretold. Many regarded the coming Messiah as the only one who could fulfill these words, as is evident from the fact that Simeon, who had been given the assurance that he would not die before he had seen the Messiah, quoted from Isaiah 42:6 and 49:6 as he held the baby Jesus in his arms (Luke 2:27-32). It is instructive to notice the full text of the Scripture quoted in part by Simeon:

"I am the LORD, I have called you in righteousness. I will also hold you by the hand and watch over you, And I will appoint you as a covenant to the people, As a light to the nations" (Isa. 42:6).
And now says the LORD, who formed Me from the womb to be His Servant, To bring Jacob back to Him, in order that Israel might be gathered to Him (For I am honored in the sight of the LORD, And My God is My strength). He says, "It is too small a thing that You should be My Servant To raise up the tribes of Jacob, and to restore the preserved ones of Israel; I will also make You a light of the nations So that My salvation may reach to the end of the earth" (Isa. 49:5-6).

Jesus had steeped his soul in these glorious Scriptures in which he heard his Father speaking directly to him. The suffering was there and could not be avoided. It was God's will for his Servant, the Messiah. But the glory was there also, and the worldwide task. Jesus accepted the cup of suffering and endured the cross, knowing that it was not only for the lost sheep of the house of Israel, but for all the nations who were to be called to repentance in his name.

Jeremiah and the Nations

Jeremiah was fully aware that he was called not only to speak to the people of Israel but to be "a prophet to the nations" (Jer. 1:5). The latter part of his book contains messages of warning and judgment addressed to Egypt (Jer. 46), Philistia (Jer. 47), Moab (Jer. 48), Ammon (Jer. 49), and Babylon (Jer. 50-51). But the chief burden of Jeremiah was for the unfaithful nation of Judah, the Southern Kingdom sometimes also referred to as Israel. He was appointed to denounce the disobedient nation and explain why God was bringing the Babylonians to punish them, in spite of their many sacrifices offered at the Temple and their pious claims to be God's Chosen People. God spoke through Jeremiah:

For I did not speak to your fathers, or command them in the day that I brought them out of the land of Egypt, concerning burnt offerings and sacrifices. But this is what I commanded them, saying, "Obey My voice, and I will be your God, and you will be My people; and you will walk in all the way which I command you, that it may be well with you." "Yet they did not obey or incline their ear, but walked in their own counsels and in the stubbornness of their evil heart, and went backward and not forward. Since the day that your fathers came out of the land of Egypt until this day, I have sent you all My servants the prophets, daily rising early and sending them. Yet they did not listen to Me or incline their ear, but stiffened their neck; they did evil more than their fathers . . . .

And you shall say to them, "This is the nation that did

not obey the voice of the LORD their God or accept correction; truth has perished and has been cut off from their mouth" (Jer. 7:22-28).

Jeremiah gave assurance that the nation was not completely rejected by God, and that a remnant would be spared and allowed to return and rebuild Jerusalem (Jer. 23:3-5). He foresaw a glorious day when a new covenant would be made with the house of Israel to replace the old covenant which had been broken:

"But this is the covenant which I will make with the house of Israel after those days," declares the LORD, "I will put My law within them, and on their heart I will write it; and I will be their God, and they shall be My people. And they shall not teach again, each man his neighbor and each man his brother, saying, 'Know the LORD,' for they shall all know Me, from the least of them to the greatest of them," declares the LORD, "for I will forgive their iniquity, and their sin I will remember no more" (Jer. 31:33-34).

God's ultimate purpose for the nations, to be achieved in part through his Chosen People, is stated clearly in Jeremiah 16:19-21:

O LORD, my strength and my stronghold,   And my refuge in the day of distress,   To Thee the nations will come   From the ends of the earth and say,   "Our fathers have inherited nothing but falsehood,   Futility and things of no profit."   Can man make gods for himself?   Yet they are not gods!
Therefore behold, I am going to make them know—   This time I will make them know   My power and My might; And they shall know that My name is the LORD.

Ezekiel and the Nations

Ezekiel's messages were directed primarily to the exiles in Babylon, to whom he explained that the downfall of the nation had been because of sin and disobedience.

He assured them that a remnant would be allowed to return, and that in the future each individual would be judged on the basis of his own deeds, and not those of his father or of the nation as a whole (Ezek. 18). He had words of warning for the nations of Ammon, Moab, Edom, Philistia, Tyre, Sidon, and Egypt (Ezek. 25—32). But his harshest judgments were against the leaders of Israel, described as shepherds who did not feed the flock, but allowed the sheep to be scattered and lost. Ezekiel 34 forms the background for Jesus' words in John 10, in which he pictures himself as the Good Shepherd.

Ezekiel 36 makes clear why judgment came upon Judah during the Babylonian captivity, and reveals the ultimate purpose God will accomplish in bringing back the captives, in order that his glory might be known among the nations:

Therefore, say to the house of Israel, Thus says the Lord GOD, "It is not for your sake, O house of Israel, that I am about to act, but for My holy name, which you have profaned among the nations where you went. And I will vindicate the holiness of My great name which has been profaned among the nations, which you have profaned in their midst. Then the nations will know that I am the LORD," declares the Lord GOD, "when I prove Myself holy among you in their sight" (Ezek. 36:22-23).

Again and again the determined intention is declared:

And I shall magnify Myself, sanctify Myself, and make Myself known in the sight of many nations; and they will know that I am the LORD (Ezek. 38:23).

And My holy name I shall make known in the midst of My people Israel; and I shall not let My holy name be profaned any more. And the nations will know that I am the LORD, the Holy One in Israel (Ezek. 39:7).

Hosea and Amos

The book of Daniel is not included among the Prophets in the Hebrew Bible, but in the third section, The Writings. Its influence on the ministry of Jesus will be considered in a later chapter.

Hosea and Amos both preached to the Northern Kingdom shortly before it was overrun by the Assyrians in 722 B.C. Their words stand as a warning that Yahweh is the eternal God of all nations, not a national deity whose love and concern are limited to Israel; and that judgment will fall upon any generation which disobeys and breaks the covenant. The certainty of judgment upon the Northern Kingdom was dramatized by Hosea in names which he gave to his children. A daughter was called "Lo-ruhamah," which means literally, "No-mercy." It was an unusual name, and Hosea was instructed to take every opportunity to explain why God had given her this name. When anyone asked why the child was called "No-mercy," the rugged prophet replied, "Because God has declared, 'I will have *no mercy* upon the house of Israel' " (Hos. 1:6).

Later a boy was born and named "Lo-ammi," which means "Not-My-people." Again, as the people inquired why this strange name, the prophet would answer, "Because God says, 'You are *not My people,* and I am not your God' " (Hos. 1:9).

Hosea, who is known as the brokenhearted prophet, sadly predicted that the Northern Kingdom would be utterly destroyed. This came about in 722 B.C. when Sargon of Assyria devastated the land and carried captive the king and all the noblemen, leaving only some of the peasant class. These intermarried with their conquerors and with other local people and became the Samaritans, a mixed race despised by the Judeans to the south, who desperately sought to preserve their racial purity. The Northern Kingdom was never restored, and "the lost ten tribes of Israel" became a legend. The name "Israel" was later applied to the restored Southern Kingdom, which had long been known as "Judah"; but the old Israel, with its capital at Samaria, had not been restored at the time of Jesus. It had indeed ceased to be the People of God, because of disobedience.

Paul quotes Hosea 1:10 and 23 [2:23] as beginning to be fulfilled when Gentiles, who had not been the people of God become "My People" and pagan tribes who had not received mercy find God's mercy in the gospel of Christ (Rom. 9:25-26). Not in the restoration of Israel as a nation but in the new spiritual Israel, Hosea's hopes and longings were at last to be fulfilled.

Amos also preached to the Northern Kingdom, although he was himself a southerner from Tekoa near Jerusalem. His fiery sermon was delivered at Bethel, the religious center of Israel. It is a masterpiece of eloquence as the prophet announces God's judgment upon nation after nation and moves to a dramatic climax in his denunciation of Israel. The stern denunciation of Damascus won a hearing and perhaps applause, since the Syrians were age-long enemies of Israel. Then in rapid succession Gaza, to the southwest, was condemned, followed by Tyre to the northwest, and Edom, far south of Israel. Ammon and Moab were closer, yet deserved the punishment which Amos announced, his listeners believed. To their surprise, the prophet then denounced Judah, his own country, "because they have despised the law of the Lord, and have not kept his commandments" (Amos

2:4, KJV). This came dangerously close, and the people
of Judah were cousins of the Israelites. Yet they were
wicked, and perhaps the prophet was right! God would
punish Judah! But the surprise came with the final blast
of Amos:

Thus says the LORD, "For three transgressions of Israel and
for four I will not revoke its punishment, Because they sell
the righteous for money And the needy for a pair of sandals"
(Amos 2:6).

This was too much! The proud people of Israel were
offended and violently rejected the message. They would
not believe that God would punish them, his own Chosen
People! Amos was sternly commanded to go back to his
home in Judah, and preach no more in Israel. Amos left,
but not until he gave one final word of warning: Israel
would fall and never rise up again (Amos 8:14).

Amos recognized that Israel had been chosen by God
as his covenant people. But he pointed out that privilege
brings responsibility. God's word to Israel was: "You only
have I known of all the families of the earth; therefore
I will punish you for all your iniquities" (Amos 3:2, RSV).

The principle of God's control over all nations, and
the fact that his choice of Israel was not on the basis
of favoritism and partiality was clearly stated by Amos.
If Israel disobeyed, it must come under the righteous
judgment of God, who dealt with all peoples justly:

"Are you not as the sons of Ethiopia to Me, O sons of
Israel?" declares the LORD. "Have I not brought up Israel
from the land of Egypt, and the Philistines from Caphtor
and the Syrians from Kir? "Behold, the eyes of the Lord God
are on the sinful kingdom, And I will destroy it from the
face of the earth; Nevertheless, I will not totally destroy the
house of Jacob," Declares the LORD (Amos 9:7-8).

The last clause, almost as an afterthought, gives a ray of hope, which is more fully revealed in Amos 9:11-12:

"In that day I will raise up the fallen booth of David, And wall up its breaches;   I will also raise up its ruins,   And rebuild it as in the days of old;   That they may possess the remnant of Edom   And all the nations who are called by My name,"   Declares the LORD who does this.

Eight hundred years later at the Jerusalem Conference (Acts 15), James, the leader of the Jerusalem church, quoted this passage from Amos, seeing its fulfillment in the conversion of the Gentiles. His quotation is from the Greek Septuagint, which makes even stronger the universal tone. Instead of "Edom," as in the Hebrew text used by our translators, the Greek translated "Adam," which means "mankind," probably from another version of the Hebrew. As James explained, God's ultimate purpose through Israel was not defeated even with the fall of Samaria and the end of the Northern Kingdom. Now at last it was beginning to be fulfilled as Gentiles were coming to Christ, the Messiah. The purpose as James read it from Amos is: "IN ORDER THAT THE REST OF MANKIND MAY SEEK THE LORD,   AND ALL THE GENTILES WHO ARE CALLED BY MY NAME," SAYS THE LORD, WHO MAKES THESE THINGS KNOWN FROM OF OLD (Acts 15:17-18).

Joel's Call for Universal Repentance

Joel's brief prophecy was delivered to Judah at the time of a great plague of locusts and caterpillars. The prophet saw this as judgment of God upon the wicked nation, and urged repentance in order to avoid even greater destruction. He warned: "The day of the Lord is near,

And it will come as destruction from the Almighty" (Joel 1:15).

Judgment would come first upon Judah, and then upon all the Gentile nations (Joel 3:2, 9-14). The message was the same for all: "Whoever calls on the name of the Lord Will be delivered" (Joel 2:32).

Peter quoted Joel 2:28-32 on the day of Pentecost, declaring that this was the beginning of the fulfillment of the promised outpouring of the spirit "UPON ALL MANKIND" (Acts 2:17). The Hebrew term is "all flesh," which is sweepingly inclusive as is the word *whoever*. Paul quoted Joel 2:32 in his letter to the Romans (10:13), and specifically affirmed that "WHOEVER" means Jews and Gentiles, without any distinction. This has become the "whosoever" of the gospel, first declared by the prophet Joel.

Micah's Hope for Peace

Micah's universalism is well-known. He first announced the doom of the Northern Kingdom: "For I will make Samaria a heap of ruins in the open country, . . . For her wound is incurable" (Mic. 1:6,9). Jerusalem also was marked for destruction (v. 12), but afterward would be restored, and ultimately become a glorious center of international blessing and peace:

> And it will come about in the last days
> That the mountain of the house of the LORD
> Will be established as the chief of the mountains.
> It will be raised above the hills,
> And the peoples will stream to it.
> And many nations will come and say,
> "Come and let us go up to the mountain of the LORD
> And to the house of the God of Jacob,
> That He may teach us about His ways
> And that we may walk in His paths."

> For from Zion will go forth the law,
> Even the word of the LORD from Jerusalem.
> And He will judge between many peoples
> And render decisions for mighty, distant nations.
> Then they will hammer their swords into plowshares
> And their spears into pruning hooks;
> Nation will not lift up sword against nation,
> And never again will they train for war (Mic. 4:1-3).

This vision of a time of universal peace Micah shared with Isaiah (2:2-4). But the prediction that Bethlehem would be the birthplace of One who would not only be a ruler in Israel, but would be great "to the ends of the earth" and the source of peace for all is distinctive of Micah (5:2-5).

Habakkuk's World Vision

Habakkuk proclaimed God as the ruler of all nations, who raised up the Chaldeans to punish wayward Judah. He declared the universal principle, "the righteous will live by his faith" (Hab. 2:4), which was to be cherished later by Paul (Rom. 1:17; Gal. 3:11) and by Luther. He predicted a day when "The earth will be filled With the knowledge of the glory of the LORD,   As the waters cover the sea" (Hab. 2:14). His call for universal worship has never been excelled: "The LORD is in His holy temple. Let all the earth be silent before Him" (Hab. 2:20).

Zechariah and Jesus

How much Jesus was influenced by the universal theme which was so prominent in the prophets we cannot determine. But just as surely as he regarded himself as the Suffering Servant of Isaiah, so he most certainly believed that he was the righteous king promised by Zechariah.

Indeed, he deliberately arranged for his "Triumphal entry" into Jerusalem in order to fulfill the words of Zechariah 9:9:

> Rejoice greatly, O daughter of Zion!
> Shout in triumph, O daughter of Jerusalem!
> Behold, your king is coming to you;
> He is just and endowed with salvation,
> Humble, and mounted on a donkey,
> Even on a colt, the foal of a donkey.

It is inconceivable that Jesus was not keenly aware also of the verse which follows:

> And I will cut off the chariot from Ephraim,
> And the horse from Jerusalem;
> And the bow of war will be cut off.
> And He will speak peace to the nations;
> And His dominion will be from sea to sea,
> And from the River to the ends of the earth
> (Zech. 9:10).

Jesus must also have been mindful of the glorious expectation expressed in Zechariah 8:20-23:

> Thus says the LORD of hosts, "It will yet be that peoples will come, even the inhabitants of many cities; and the inhabitants of one will go to another saying, "Let us go at once to entreat the favor of the LORD, and to seek the Lord of hosts; I will also go."
> "So many peoples and mighty nations will come to seek the LORD of hosts in Jerusalem and entreat the favor of the Lord."
> Thus says the LORD of hosts, "In those days ten men from the nations of every language will grasp the garment of a Jew saying, 'Let us go with you, for we have heard that God is with you.'"

This could only be accomplished by his suffering and death. He must fulfill these words of the prophet Zechariah: "They will look on Me whom they have pierced" (Zech. 12:10); "In that day a fountain will be opened for the house of David and for the inhabitants of Jerusalem, for sin and for impurity" (Zech. 13:1); "And one will say to him, 'What are these wounds between your arms?' Then he will say, 'Those with which I was wounded in the house of my friends'" (Zech. 13:6); and "Strike the Shepherd that the sheep may be scattered" (Zech. 13:7).

But Jesus knew that his suffering would not be in vain, for he had read Zechariah to the end and was confident that "it will come about in that day that living waters will flow out of Jerusalem . . . And the LORD will be king over all the earth; in that day the LORD will be the only one, and His name the only one" (Zech. 14:8-9). And after many trials and tribulations, "Then it will come about that any who are left of all the nations that went against Jerusalem will go up from year to year to worship the King, the LORD of hosts, and to celebrate the Feast of Booths. And it will be that whichever of the families of the earth does not go up to Jerusalem to worship the King, the LORD of hosts, there will be no rain on them" (Zech. 14:16-17). Distinctions between the sacred and the secular will be wiped out, as commonplace articles will be sanctified and the glory of the LORD will be everywhere:

In that day there will be inscribed on the bells of the horses, "HOLY TO THE LORD." And the cooking pots in the LORD's house will be like the bowls before the altar. And every cooking pot in Jerusalem and in Judah will be holy to the LORD of hosts; and all who sacrifice will come and take of them and boil in them. And there will no longer be a Canaanite in the house of the LORD of hosts in that day (Zech. 14:20-21).

The message of the prophets was unmistakable. Yahweh, the eternal One is the God of all nations. All will be judged with righteousness and justice. The call for repentance is universal. The Messiah must suffer for all, and after his resurrection repentance as a basis for forgiveness of sins must be proclaimed to all the nations.

Jesus knew how to read the Bible. He received the message of the prophets, planned his ministry on that basis, and then interpreted the message and the ministry to his disciples, saying, "Thus it is written, that the Messiah must suffer and rise again from the dead the third day; and that repentance for forgiveness of sins must be proclaimed in His name to all the nations, beginning from Jerusalem" (Luke 24:46-47, author's translation).

Notes

[1] See commentary by Page H. Kelley in *The Broadman Bible Commentary*, volume 5 (Nashville: Broadman Press, 1971), p. 341.

[2] Isaiah 54:2-3. This is the text used by William Carey for his famous sermon in 1792, which resulted in the formation of the Baptist Missionary Society.

IV.
All Nations in the Psalms

The book of Psalms was the Hebrew hymnbook. Its hymns of praise were chanted during worship services at the Temple, and recited in synagogues and in the homes of the faithful. While some of the psalms are purely personal, individual confessions and prayers for assistance, many are congregational, corporate expressions of praise by the people of Israel. A surprising number are universalistic, calling for all the peoples of the world to worship and honor Yahweh, the God of Israel, as the king of all the earth. Some indeed are missionary in nature, exhorting the people of God to bear their testimony to the heathen nations, in order that the eternal purpose of God may be achieved and the one true God may be worshiped by every living thing on earth.

Unfortunately, this universal note has been obscured in the King James Version, primarily because of the way one Hebrew word is translated. The word *am* means "people"; that is, a group of individuals having a corporate identity, as for example, the people of Israel, or the people of Syria. The Hebrew language forms the plural by adding *im,* which is the equivalent of "s" added to an English word. When the word *ammim* occurs, it should always be translated "peoples," since it refers to more than one group. It usually means the other peoples, or nations, as compared with the people of Israel, which is commonly designated by the singular word, *am.* The English word *people* is a collective plural, referring to more than one person, but it can also mean one group of persons, unless the "s" is added.

In Psalm 47:1, for example, the King James Version reads: "O clap your hands, all ye people; shout unto God with the voice of triumph." This could be thought of as a call to all the people of Israel to rejoice and worship God. But the correct translation is: "Clap your hands, all peoples! Shout to God with loud songs of joy!" (Ps. 47:1, RSV). This is obviously addressed to all the nations, calling upon them to join the people of Israel in worship of the one true God.

Another example is Psalm 96:3, which in the King James Version is rendered: "Declare his glory among the heathen, his wonders among all people." Here the Hebrew word *goyim,* another plural, is translated "heathen," whereas "nations" would be more appropriate. The exhortation for God's people to witness to the other peoples of the earth is more clearly expressed in these words: "Declare his glory among the nations, his marvelous works among all the peoples!" (Ps. 96:3, RSV).

Likewise in Psalm 96:13 the universal role of God as judge of all the nations is softened somewhat in the King James translation: "He shall judge the world with righteousness, and the people with his truth." It is made clear when the plural is used:

> He will judge the world with righteousness,
> and the peoples with his truth" (Ps. 96:13, RSV).

Other verses in which it is important to read "peoples" instead of "people" are:

Bless our God, O peoples,
  let the sound of his praise be heard (Ps. 66:8, RSV).

O give thanks to the Lord, call on his name,
  make known his deeds among the peoples (Ps. 105:1,
  RSV).

Praise the Lord, all nations!
Extol him, all peoples! (Ps. 117:1, RSV).

Psalm 67:3 takes on new meaning when the plural is emphasized:

Let the peoples praise thee, O God;
  let all the peoples praise thee (RSV).

"Let all the people praise thee," as in the King James Version, could mean, "Let all the Hebrew people praise thee." But the entire psalm is a prayer for God to continue his blessing upon his Chosen People for a specific purpose: "That thy way may be known upon earth, thy saving power among all nations" (Ps. 67:2, RSV). His people dare to ask God, who has blessed them so many times, to bless them again, so that they in turn may be a blessing to other nations and that finally all the ends of the earth may fear and worship him, as expressed in the last verse of the psalm.

Regrettably, it is to be feared that some readers of the King James Version have been encouraged to place the same limitations upon these psalms as the Jewish people apparently did much of the time. Although the inspired hymns were addressed to all the nations of the earth, calling upon them to join in the worship of the one true God, they were sung by the people of Israel as though they were intended for them in some exclusive way. They knew better, for they understood the difference between *am* and *ammim,* the people and the peoples.

But they chanted their hymns within the Temple at Jerusalem, and the nations to whom so many of the psalms were directed could not hear the call to universal worship.

In similar fashion, worshiping congregations today often sing heartily some missionary hymn such as "Send the Light," or "O Zion, Haste," and then do little to project the sound of praise beyond the four walls of the church. Perhaps the use of the new translations of the Bible will make plain the worldwide audience for which these psalms were written, and help Christians avoid the narrowness and parochialism which afflicted the Jews of Jesus' day.

Jesus knew the psalms well. From those with a universal note he doubtless had received inspiration and the impulse to call all the peoples of the earth to worship the one true God. From them he had the assurance that God would judge all nations with equity and righteousness. More than that, he knew that he was the Messiah, God's anointed king, through whom God would deal with the nations in a world-encompassing work of judgment and redemption.

Many of the psalms which were regarded as Messianic in Jesus' day had originally referred to David or some other Hebrew king. Poetical language was used to compliment the ruler and idealize his influence and honor among the nations of the world. No king in the past had ever realized in full the promises of the inspired psalmists, and the hope now was for a golden age in the future. For years there had been no legitimate Davidic king in Jerusalem. The Herods were regarded as impostors and Judah was under Gentile rule. Devout Jews longed for a restoration of the Davidic line and with it the glory and honor that their nation had once enjoyed among the nations of the world. They knew that this could take place only when God sent his chosen Anointed One. The expectation was keen at the time of Jesus, and many scriptures were used to support the messianic hope.

Jesus' Use of the Psalms

When Jesus entered Jerusalem on "Palm Sunday," he was greeted by the multitudes with the cry, "BLESSED IS THE ONE WHO COMES IN THE NAME OF THE LORD" (Matt. 21:9). This was a direct quotation from Psalm 118:26. It was acknowledged by Jesus as the recognition that he was indeed "the Son of David," the promised King (just as his riding on the back of a donkey was a deliberate fulfillment of Zech. 9:9). He accepted the acclamation of the children, "Hosanna to the Son of David" (Matt. 21:15), and in answer to the indignation of the chief priests and scribes, Jesus quoted from Psalm 8:2, as evidence that it was proper for him to accept their praise as God's representative. His quotation is from the Greek Septuagint, which is even stronger than the Hebrew text:

> OUT OF THE MOUTHS OF INFANTS AND NURS-ING BABES THOU HAS PREPARED PRAISE FOR THYSELF (Matt. 21:16).

But Jesus knew that he was not to be an ordinary political king. He also knew that he would be rejected by the official leaders of the nation. In the Temple a few days later he quoted from the same psalm with which he had been greeted on Sunday: "The stone which the builders rejected has become the chief corner *stone*. This is the Lord's doing; it is marvelous in our eyes" (Ps. 118:22-23). This pointed not only to his rejection, but beyond that to his vindication and triumph. In the same psalm he found words which brought to his heart the assurance of ultimate victory:

> I shall not die, but live,
> And tell of the works of the Lord.
> The Lord has disciplined me severely,
> But He has not given me over to death
>
> (Ps. 118:17-18).

No one had ever seen in these verses the meaning which they had for Jesus. He put them together and almost surely interpreted them to his disciples for the first time on the evening of the resurrection day.

Jesus acknowledged the title, "Son of David," the popular designation of the expected Messiah. But he did not really like it. His personal choice of a title for himself was "Son of man," which identified him with all humanity, rather than with the Jewish people in a narrow, nationalistic sense. We shall note later the source of that title and its full significance. Matthew 22:41-46 describes how he challenged the appropriateness of the term "Son of David" as applied to the Messiah. For this purpose he used Psalm 110, which was accepted by his hearers as a messianic psalm written by David himself. Let us paraphrase his conversation with the Pharisees:

"What about the Messiah?" he asked. "Whose son is he?" When they answered "David's," Jesus retorted, "Why is it then that David, in the inspired psalm which he wrote, says of the Messiah, "Yahweh said to my Lord, 'Sit at my right hand until I put your enemies under your feet'? You see, David himself calls the Messiah "my Lord," recognizing that the Messiah is superior to him. Why then should the Messiah be called 'the son of

David,' which implies that he is inferior to David (since a son is under his father)?"

This bold statement, based upon the rabbinical method of interpreting Scripture, stopped the questioning of the Pharisees. It also showed clearly that Jesus considered himself, as the Messiah, to be above the political schemes of those who looked for a nationalistic messiah to overthrow the hated Roman rule and reestablish an independent Jewish kingdom.

Since it is obvious that Jesus regarded Psalm 110 as an inspired prophecy of the Messiah, we do well to note its full content. The word LORD printed in capital letters in verses 1, 2, and 4 is a translation of the Hebrew YHWH, the sacred personal name of God, written only with the consonants, according to Hebrew custom. Considered too sacred to be pronounced, it was replaced by the word *Adonai* in oral reading. To aid readers, the vowels of *Adonai* were written with the consonants of YHWH in the Masoretic text. These letters transliterated produced the word *Jehovah*, which has been used in some versions of the Bible, but which is a hybrid word. "Yahweh" is closer to the original Hebrew pronunciation.

The second word *Lord* in Psalm 110:1 and 5, not printed in capitals, is a translation of *Adonai* "my lord" and in this context does not refer to God himself, but to the Messiah. To emphasize this, the Revised Standard Version prints the first line of this psalm: "The LORD says to my lord." The meaning is "Yahweh (God) says to my lord (the Messiah)." Thus Jesus would read this to mean that God the Father promised to Christ the Son a place of honor until all his enemies are overcome.

Likewise, in verse 4 Yahweh (God the Father) promised

to make the Messiah a priest forever after the order of Melchizedek, and in verse 5, it is the Messiah ("the Lord" not capitalized, not Yahweh) who will shatter rebellious kings and execute judgment among the nations. There can be no doubt that Jesus expected to fulfill this role. He realized that the victory over the nations was not to be accomplished by military might. It was to be a spiritual victory. "My kingship is not of this world," he said. "If my kingship were of this world, my servants would fight . . . but my kingship is not from the world" (John 18:36, RSV). Thus he would not consent to be the kind of Messiah the people were expecting. But he did claim to be a king, the messianic king, and he knew that as such he was to be the judge of the nations and to exercise an eternal priesthood. For what was written of him in Psalm 110 must be fulfilled.

Psalm 2

Although Jesus never quoted the second Psalm, so far as is recorded, there can be no doubt that he read it as applying to himself as the Messiah. The Jerusalem church made this identification soon after Pentecost, as seen in Acts 4:25-28. The psalm was widely regarded as messianic and was the subject of commentary by several ancient rabbis.[1] The reason is obvious. In verse 2 the word translated "anointed" is the Hebrew word *meshiach,* from which comes the English word "Messiah." The word translated "the LORD" is again the Hebrew YHWH. Thus it is Yahweh (God) and his anointed King who see the nations and kings of the earth plotting rebellion against them. Whatever may have been its meaning in earlier times, in the day of Jesus this psalm pointed to the coming Messiah.

In verses 4 and 5 the psalmist supposes that God will merely laugh at the rebellious nations and punish them in his wrath. But it is not that simple. God has a plan. In verse 6 God himself speaks, declaring that he will deal with the nations of the earth through his messianic king, the Messiah. At verse 7 the Messiah speaks, saying, "Let me explain the announced plan of Yahweh. He has said to me, 'You are my Son. Today I have become your Father. Ask me, and I will give you the nations as an inheritance. Indeed, I will give you the very ends of the earth for your possession" (author's paraphrase).

The psalmist, following this exposition by the Messiah, turns and addresses the rulers of the Gentile nations, urging them to be wise and save themselves from judgment and destruction by being reconciled to the Messiah and granting reverent worship to God. Verse 12 translated literally reads, "Kiss the Son, lest he be angry." The kiss is a symbol of reconciliation. The Son is obviously the Messiah. Jesus knew that it referred in prophetic symbolism to him. The nations were called upon to repent and be reconciled to God through the Messiah.

At the time of his baptism, Jesus heard a voice from heaven saying, "This is My beloved Son, in whom I am well pleased" (Matt. 3:17). This was an echo of Psalm 2:7. No other Scripture applies the title "Son of God" so clearly to the Messiah. It spoke directly to the heart of Jesus, confirming his own deep inner consciousness of a unique relationship of sonship to his heavenly Father. When the devil had shown him all the kingdoms of the world and offered to give them to him, if he would fall down and worhip Satan, Jesus answered with a verse from Deuteronomy 6:13. He could also have quoted Psalm 2:8, with the retort: "The kingdoms are not really yours to give. My Father has said, 'Ask of me, and I will give you the nations as an inheritance! I shall receive them from him, and not from you!' " (author's theoretical wording).

Later in his risen form he told his disciples, "You shall be My witnesses both in Jerusalem, and in all Judea and Samaria, and even to the remotest part of the earth" (Acts 1:8). This is an echo of Psalm 2:8, with its promise concerning "the uttermost parts of the earth." From this messianic psalm he had the assurance that his spiritual kingdom would be worldwide in its extent, and this he explained to his disciples on the resurrection day.

Psalm 22

"ELI, ELI, LAMA SABACHTHANI?" These words are a direct quotation from Psalm 22:1 in Hebrew. Matthew 27:46 gives the translation: "MY GOD, MY GOD, WHY HAST THOU FORSAKEN ME?" This has been called "the cry of dereliction," and it is commonly assumed that Jesus went no further in his quotation of the psalm. While no other verses are recorded and he perhaps did not quote others audibly, there is a distinct possibility that Jesus may have recited to himself as he hung on the cross all thirty-one verses of this magnificent poem, which is almost unbelievable in its inspired quality. If not on the cross, it is quite likely that he interpreted the entire psalm to his disciples after his resurrection.

Psalm 22 falls into three main sections. The first twenty-one verses are the cry of anguish from one suffering great pain of body and soul. It reads almost like an eyewitness account of the crucifixion. The taunting crowd, the awful thirst, the enemies casting lots for his garments—it is all there. It is easy to imagine Jesus silently quoting to himself from memory those awful words, and reflecting, "Now indeed is this scripture being fulfilled."

But it is important to notice that the psalm does not end at verse 21. There is a definite transition in the latter part of that verse. The Hebrew text seems to be uncertain and there are several variant readings. If the ancient Greek and Syriac texts are accepted, and the last four words of Psalm 22:21 are placed at the beginning of verse 22, the passage reads as follows:

> Save me from the lion's mouth;
> And from the horns of the wild oxen.
>
> Thou dost answer me!
> I will tell of Thy name to my brethren;
> In the midst of the assembly I will praise Thee.

This second section of the psalm continues through the first half of verse 26. It expresses the assurance that God has heard the cry of his Suffering Servant, who gives praise to God and dedicates his life anew.

At 26*b* comes another surprising transition! Beginning with the words, "Let your heart live forever!" God himself speaks to his servant, assuring him that his suffering has not been in vain. As a result, "All the ends of the earth will remember and turn to the LORD (Yahweh), and all the families of the nations will worship before Thee (the Messiah). For the Kingdom is the LORD's (Yahweh's), and He rules over the nations" (author's words).

The last three verses proclaim these sweeping truths: Both the rich and the poor will worship God because of what has been done by the Suffering Servant. Even those so impoverished that they can scarcely keep soul and body together will bow before this one and worship him. Unborn generations will serve him. The good news will be passed on to future generations. Concerning the Lord (not *Yahweh* in verse 30, but *Adonai*—not the Father God, but the Messiah, his Son) it will be declared: "He has done it!"

Just before his death on the cross, Jesus cried out, "It is finished!" (John 19:30). We gratefully thank God for "the finished work of Christ." By some miracle of inspiration, the author of Psalm 22 had peered down the centuries and had written, "To a people yet to be born it will be proclaimed, 'He has done it!' " (v. 31, author's words).

Some of us like to believe that Jesus knew Psalm 22 from beginning to end and felt that it was all written of him. Even in his suffering, he was sustained by the faith that God would keep his promises. And when he had finished his work of redemption and had been raised from the dead, he explained it all to his followers. He had done all of it "according to the Scriptures" as it was written in Moses, the Prophets, and the Psalms, and now it was up to them to tell it to all the nations.

Note

[1] Alfred Edersheim, *The Life and Times of Jesus the Messiah,* Volume II (Grand Rapids: Wm. B. Eerdman's Publishing Co., 1950), pp. 716 f.

V.
Jesus and the Gentiles

We have tried to read our Bible as Jesus read his. This took us quickly through the Old Testament, the only Scriptures Jesus had. In all three sections of the Hebrew Bible, the books of Moses, the Prophets, and the Psalms, we found God's concern for all the nations and peoples of the earth, and his plan for dealing with them through the Messiah. We believe that Jesus mentally "underscored" these passages in his Bible, and planned deliberately to fulfill them by his life, his death, and his resurrection.

Turning now to the New Testament, we find in the Gospels that the words and actions of Jesus confirm this all-inclusive concept of his ministry. The New Testament flows right out of the Old, with unbroken continuity. In the distinctive title he chose for himself, in the strategy of his ministry, and in his clear teachings, it is obvious that Jesus undertook a mission for all mankind.

Malachi and Matthew

In our Bible the Gospel of Matthew comes immediately after Malachi, and appropriately so. Whatever the date of this last of the prophets, at least two or three centuries of silence come between the Testaments. No clear word from God to his people is on record later than Malachi.

Yet, as one closes the Old Testament and opens the New, it is as though just a few days intervened. Matthew begins right where Malachi ended. And no one was more conscious of that than Jesus was. He knew that he had come to fulfill what Malachi had predicted.

The four short chapters of Malachi are an unrelieved denunciation of the nation of Israel, the warning of an imminent day of judgment to be announced by a forerunner and then instituted by "the messenger of the covenant," who would come suddenly to the Temple and inaugurate a new era, not only for the people of Israel, but for the whole world.

The coming judgment was called "the Day of the Lord." It would be "a great and terrible day" of testing, when the righteous would be separated from the wicked as gold is refined in a smelter, as dirt is removed from clothing by caustic lye soap, as chaff is separated from wheat at the threshing-floor, and as an unfruitful tree is chopped down and consumed in a furnace (Mal. 3:2; 4:1,5).

The judgment would be particularly severe on Israel and its leaders because of specific sins which are denounced: sham and hypocrisy in worship services (1:7-14); social injustice (2:10); pagan religious practices (2:11); divorce (2:16); withholding the tithe (3:8-10). But above all, the prophet declares, God's patience is coming to an end because the people who were supposed to exalt Yahweh and cause him to be reverenced and worshiped among the nations of the world have failed to do so. Instead, they have profaned his name and caused him to be dishonored (1:5-14). But God's purpose will not be defeated; for from east to west, all over the world, his name is to be exalted among the nations, and in every place prayers and worship are to be offered to him (1:11).

The keynote is sounded in Malachi 1:10-11:

"Oh that there were one among you who would shut the gates, that you might not uselessly kindle fire on My altar! I am not pleased with you," says the LORD of hosts, "nor will I accept an offering from you.

"For from the rising of the sun, even to its setting, My name will be great among the nations, and in every place incense is going to be offered to My name, and a grain offering that is pure; for My name will be great among the nations," says the LORD of hosts.

Because God is so concerned that he be exalted among the nations, he is about to act, Malachi warns. He will first send a messenger to prepare the way for him (Mal. 3:1). Then he will come himself, as the messenger of the covenant, who will inaugurate the time of judgment (Mal. 3:2-3). The forerunner will be an "Elijah," a fiery prophet of doom (Mal. 4:5). If he is not heeded, then fierce judgment and destruction will be certain.

All of these elements of Malachi are reflected in the third chapter of Matthew's Gospel. John the Baptist came preaching, "Repent, for the kingdom of heaven is at hand" (Matt. 3:2). This is the equivalent of "the Day of the Lord" in Malachi. The time of God's judgment is fast approaching! This is "the wrath to come" (Matt. 3:12). John uses the same figures of speech which are found in Malachi; the wheat and chaff are to be separated, and the unfruitful tree is to be chopped down and burned. To emphasize that the judgment is to be upon the Israelites, and not just the Gentiles, as some of the Jews believed, John declared in effect: "Don't think that you will escape because you are 'sons of Abraham.' I tell you, God is not dependent upon you. He can raise up 'sons of Abraham' from these stones, if he wishes. He will use others, if you are not worthy. You will be judged and punished, regardless of your Hebrew heritage" (Matt. 3:9, author's paraphrase).

Jesus picked up this message of warning to the nation of Israel. Immediately after his baptism we are told: From that time Jesus began to preach and say: "Repent; for the kingdom of heaven is at hand" (Matt. 4:17). The essence of his message was, "Repent, before it is too late. The time is short. The day of God's judgment is at hand."

Jesus identified John the Baptist as the Elijah whom Malachi had promised. Just after John's imprisonment, Jesus declared: "For all the prophets and the Law prophesied until John; and if you are willing to accept it, he is Elijah who is to come. He who has ears to hear, let him hear" (Matt. 11:13-15, RSV).

Jesus was warning that a turning point in history was at hand. The last of the prophets had been sent to give a final warning before judgment came upon the nation of Israel. Some months later, after the death of John the Baptist, he again identified John as the Elijah foretold by Malachi:

"But I say to you, that Elijah already came, and they did not recognize him, but did to him whatever they wished. So also the Son of Man is going to suffer at their hands." Then the disciples understood that He had spoken to them about John the Baptist (Matt. 17:12-13).

During his last week in Jerusalem as he taught in the Temple, Jesus was consciously fulfilling what is written in Malachi 3:1-2:

"Behold, I am going to send My messenger, and he will clear the way before Me. And the Lord, whom you seek, will suddenly come to His temple, and the messenger of the covenant, in whom you delight, behold, he is coming," says the LORD of hosts.

"But who can endure the day of His coming? And who can stand when He appears? For He is like a refiner's fire and like fullers' soap."

John the Baptist had been sent as a messenger to prepare the way. He had done his work. Now the Lord himself had come to announce a New Covenant to replace the Old Covenant that had been broken. ("The Lord whom you seek" is not Yahweh, but the expected Messiah, indicated by *Adon* in the Hebrew. The LORD of hosts who is announcing the coming of the Lord [*Adon*] is Yahweh. Jesus with his knowledge of Hebrew understood this distinction.) The people had been seeking the coming of the Messiah, they thought, but actually they were not ready for his coming and the judgment which it brought. Only those who were spiritually prepared could endure his coming.

This is what it means to close the Old Testament and open the New Testament. Jesus knew that the covenant made at Sinai had been broken again and again by a disobedient people, and after a long line of prophets sent to win them back had failed, God's patience was approaching an end. A new covenant was to be sealed with a faithful remnant of Israel, who would then call the Gentile nations to repentance in the name of the Messiah, the judge of the living and the dead.

Judgment must begin with the house of Israel. It then must be proclaimed to all the nations. This was the note

of urgency with which Jesus began his ministry. Matthew
fulfills Malachi!

"Son of Man"

Nothing is more revealing than the personal title which
Jesus chose for himself. We have seen that he did not
like the term, "Son of David," the popular designation
of the Messiah. He realized that he was indeed "the Son
of God" referred to in Psalm 2:7, and during his trial
before the Sanhedrin, he acknowledged this. But the title
which he used throughout his ministry was, "Son of
man." More than forty times in the Gospels the term
is used, always by Jesus referring to himself. The disciples
never used the term, but called him "Lord," "Master,"
or "Teacher." For Jesus, the words were almost a substi-
tute for the personal pronoun "I." Again and again he
said it: "The Son of Man has nowhere to lay His head"
(Matt. 8:20). "The Son of Man has authority on earth
to forgive sins" (Matt. 9:6). "The Son of Man is Lord
of the Sabbath" (Matt. 12:8). "THEN THEY SHALL SEE
THE SON OF MAN COMING IN CLOUDS with great
power and glory" (Mark 13:26).

Jesus derived this term from two principal sources: the
books of Ezekiel and Daniel. "Son of man" is the distinctive title applied to the prophet Ezekiel by God, and occurs eighty-seven times. The Hebrew is *ben Adam,* literally, "son of Adam," or "son of mankind." Originally
it meant only "man," as opposed to God, and reminded
Ezekiel of his humble status. But by the time of Jesus,
the term had become an honorific title of the Messiah,
and many passages in Ezekiel were idealized and interpreted messianically. As he read the book, Jesus must
have heard God speaking directly to him: "Son of man,

I am sending you to the sons of Israel, to a rebellious people" (Ezek. 2:3). "Son of man, I have appointed you a watchman to the house of Israel; whenever you hear a word from My mouth, warn them from Me" (3:17).

Especially significant for Jesus were the passages concerning a remnant to be spared (6:8); the new heart and spirit (11:19; 36:26-27); the divine shepherd seeking the lost sheep (34:11-16); the new everlasting covenant (37:26); and the promise that the Gentile nations would come to know the Lord, God of Israel (37:28; 38:23; 39:7). All these were to be fulfilled by him, as Son of man.

There can be no doubt that Daniel 7:13-14 was in the mind of Jesus when he used the title, "Son of man." There it was an Aramaic term, *bar enash,* instead of *ben Adam.* But the meaning is similar, *enash* being the word for mankind in general, as against an individual male person. In rabbinical commentary and popular thought, the term had already been highly spiritualized, indicating the ideal man, almost divine in nature. The Book of Enoch, an apocalyptic discourse widely circulated during the first century, exalted the figure even beyond Daniel's vision.[1] But it is not necessary to assume that Jesus was influenced by Enoch. The words of Daniel are clear enough:

> I kept looking in the night visions,
> And behold, with the clouds of heaven
> One like a Son of Man was coming,
> And He came up to the Ancient of Days
> And was presented before Him.
> And to Him was given dominion,
> Glory and a kingdom,
> That all the peoples, nations, and *men of every* lan-
>   uage
> Might serve him.

His dominion is an everlasting dominion
Which will not pass away;
And His kingdom is one
Which will not be destroyed (7:13-14).

Jesus knew that this would take place only after his suffering and glorification. He claimed the title for himself, thus identifying himself, not with the Hebrew people or the Jewish nation in any exclusive way, but with the whole human race, with all the families of mankind. He knew that he was the Son of man and the Suffering Servant.[2]

From the Beginning

As we have already seen, the vision of a universal kingdom was integral to the plan of Jesus from the very beginning of his ministry. The fact that one of the wilderness temptations involved "all the kingdoms of the world and their glory" (Matt. 4:8) is conclusive. Jesus *did* aspire to world dominion. His ambition to rule over the nations was not wrong. The temptation was to take a short cut to that noble goal: to adopt the methods of the devil. In rejecting Satan's methods, Jesus did not give up his aim of worldwide authority. Rather, he chose the path of suffering and redemption which he found outlined in the Scriptures.

The first sermon at Nazareth demonstrates that his life purpose extended far beyond the nation of Israel. He was not surprised that his own people did not receive his message. "That's the way it has always been," he said. "The prophets have always found greater faith among foreigners than among their own people" (Luke 4:24, author's paraphrase). He then gave an example: "There were many widows in Israel in the days of Elijah

. . . and yet [he] was sent to none of them, but only to Zarephath, in the land of Sidon, to a woman who was a widow" (Luke 4:25-26). His hearers knew the rest of the story told in 1 Kings 17. Received into a Gentile home, Elijah performed the remarkable miracle of replenishing the flour and oil, then later restored the widow's son to life—not a Jewish widow, but a Gentile!

Jesus did not stop with Elijah. He rubbed salt into the wounded feelings of his audience with the story of Elisha. For Naaman, the Syrian, was not only a Gentile, but a military leader—captain of the Syrian army which at that very time was at war with Israel and had almost eradicated the hapless little nation (2 Kings 5:1-14). Yet, although there were many lepers in Israel, "none of them was cleansed, but only Naaman the Syrian" (Luke 4:27). No more dramatic illustration could have been given that the grace of God was not limited to the people of Israel and that Gentiles often displayed greater faith than those who were considered "children of the kingdom." Small wonder that the proud citizens of Nazareth were infuriated at this brash young man, who insulted their nation and called in question their privileged status as God's "Chosen People"! But for his miraculous power, they would have hurled him to his death on the jagged rocks at the foot of a cliff (Luke 4:28-30).

To the Jews First

Jesus did have a deep conviction of a special mission to the Jewish nation. He expressed this so strongly that some have concluded that he envisioned no mission beyond Israel. But careful consideration of all his words and actions reveals that it was a question of strategy: As Paul later expressed it, his mission was "to the Jew first, and also to the Greek" (Rom. 1:16; 2:10).

Jesus' concern for Israel was shown in the instructions to the twelve disciples as he sent them out on their first preaching mission. "Do not go in the way of the Gentiles," he said, "and do not enter any city of the Samaritans; but rather go to the lost sheep of the house of Israel" (Matt. 10:5-6). The reason is obvious. The time was short, and doom was coming to the nation, if there was not speedy repentance. The need was urgent, more so for Israel than for the Gentile nations, whose time of judgment would come later. Indeed, in the very same context is the prediction that the preaching ministry of the disciples would be extended to the Gentiles: "You shall even be brought before governors and kings for My sake, as a testimony to the Gentiles" (v. 18). But they must concentrate upon the Jewish cities first, because their time of opportunity was short (v. 23).

Luke tells of a later preaching mission in which seventy others were sent out two by two (Luke 10:1). Just as the twelve apostles symbolically represent the twelve tribes of Israel, the seventy symbolize the Gentile nations. In Genesis 10, the descendants of Noah are listed, seventy in number. Rabbinical tradition assumed that this was the total number of nations scattered over the earth after the Tower of Babel, and repeatedly referred to the seventy Gentile peoples. Jesus may have used this means of symbolizing his long-range purpose. The twelve were sent to warn the tribes of Israel of impending judgment. The seventy were sent later on a training mission in preparation for their ultimate mission to the whole world.[3]

Contacts with Gentiles

Most of the public ministry of Jesus was conducted in Jewish territory. Under the circumstances, the number of personal contacts with Gentiles recorded in the Gospels is surprising. He healed a Gadarene demoniac (Matt. 8:28-34). Among ten lepers healed, one was a Samaritan, and Jesus remarked upon the fact that only the foreigner returned to thank him (Luke 17:12-19). A Samaritan woman was the sole audience for one of Jesus' greatest sermons. She received the assurance that the time was near when God would be worshiped, not just in Jerusalem or at Mt. Gerizim, but all over the world, "in spirit and in truth" (John 4:5-42).

A Canaanite woman's faith was rewarded when her daughter was healed. Much has been made of Jesus' puzzling remark at the beginning of the encounter: "I was sent only to the lost sheep of the house of Israel" (Matt. 15:24). This may have been a deliberate rebuke of his disciples, who had wanted to send her away with her request unanswered, and who shared the racial prejudice which was common at the time. The significant point is that Jesus *did* minister to this Gentile woman, and praised her faith in the presence of his disciples and the Jewish onlookers (v. 28).

The centurion whose servant was healed was almost certainly a Roman. Commander of a band of one hundred foreign soldiers quartered at Capernaum to keep the peace, he was despised by the Jews who resented this "army of occupation." Conscious of his own authority as a military man, he humbly assured Jesus that it would not be necessary for him to go to his house to heal the servant (and thus perhaps render himself unclean by entering a Gentile home). "Just say the word and my servant will be healed," he declared with genuine faith. Jesus turned and announced to the Jewish crowd which was following him: "I tell you the truth: I have not found a single Hebrew who showed as much faith as this Gentile military leader" (Matt. 8:10, author's paraphrase). He did not stop there, but continued with this solemn prediction: "I tell you, many such foreigners shall come from the east and the west to join Abraham, Isaac, and Jacob in the kingdom of heaven. But many others who thought they were 'sons of the kingdom' (the Chosen People of Israel) shall be shut out" (vv. 11-12, author's paraphrase).

The coming of a group of Greeks precipitated the final crisis in the inner life of Jesus: his decision to move on to the cross. It is clear that these were not merely Hellenized Jews, but aliens, either inquirers or proselytes, who had accepted Judaism and thus were qualified to worship in the Temple area, at least in the court of the Gentiles. Their request for an audience caused Jesus to declare: "The hour has come for the Son of Man to be glorified." The deep interest of the Greeks was evidence that the world was ready for his redemptive mission to be culminated by his atoning death: "And I, if I be lifted up from the earth, will draw all men to Myself." "All men"— Greeks as well as Jews; Gentiles and Hebrews alike— this is the clear implication of these profound words recorded by John (John 12:32).

The Final Week

The events of that last week in Jerusalem bear eloquent testimony to the fact that Jesus, refusing to be a nationalistic Jewish Messiah, moved resolutely toward the cross, fully aware that he was to establish a new interracial, international people, the New Israel, destined to become worldwide in its scope as a spiritual kingdom. He entered the city on a donkey, in order to fulfill Zechariah's prediction of a king who would speak peace to the nations, and whose dominion would be from sea to sea (Zech.

9:9-10). He cleansed the court of the Gentiles, declaring sternly, "MY HOUSE SHALL BE CALLED A HOUSE OF PRAYER FOR ALL THE NATIONS" (Mark 11:17). Standing in the Temple, he denounced the chief priests and Pharisees, the official leaders of the Jewish nation, for having failed to be good stewards of the truths of the Kingdom which had been entrusted to the Chosen People, and solemnly declared, "Therefore, I say unto you, the kingdom of God will be taken away from you, and given to a nation producing the fruit of it" (Matt. 21:43). He predicted the fall of Jerusalem and the destruction of the Temple within that generation (Mark 13:30; Matt. 24:34; Luke 21:32), but when asked concerning the end of the age, he said, in effect: "Don't be misled. It will not be as soon as some think. For this gospel of the Kingdom shall be preached in the whole world for a witness to all the nations, and after that the end shall come" (Matt. 24:4-14, author's paraphrase). Concerning his return in glory, he was purposely vague, declaring, "Of that day and hour no one knows, not even the angels of heaven, nor the Son, but the Father alone" (Matt. 24:36). But when he does come, he promised, "*All nations* will be gathered before Him, and He will separate them from one another, as the shepherd separates the sheep from the goats" (25:32, author's italics).

Just before the Passover, at a home in Bethany, an adoring woman anointed his body with costly ointment. When she was criticized for her extravagance, Jesus stoutly defended her with these words: "She did it to prepare Me for burial. Truly I say unto you, wherever this gospel is preached in the whole world, what this woman has done shall also be spoken of in memory of her" (26:13).

The next evening in the upper room with his disciples, he sealed the New Covenant with them, in anticipation of his death. He declared as he passed the cup, "This is My blood of the covenant, which is to be shed on behalf of many for forgiveness of sins" (v. 28). Only the eleven were present, and all were Jews. But Jesus knew that the small nucleus of a new Chosen People, the remnant of Israel, was soon to be enlarged, as the many for whom he died heard the good news and accepted him as Lord and Savior.

Notes

[1] See William Manson, *Jesus the Messiah* (London: Hodder and Stoughton, 1943), pp. 102 f.

[2] See Alfred Edersheim, *The Life and Times of Jesus the Messiah,* Vol. I, © 1950 Eerdmans, p. 173. Also for an excellent study of how Jesus combined the concept of the Son of man with that of the Suffering Servant of Isaiah, see E. A. McDowell, *Son of Man and Suffering Servant,* Broadman Press, 1944.

[3] See *The Broadman Bible Commentary,* Vol. I (Nashville: Broadman Press, 1971), p. 149.

VI.
The Commissions
of the Risen Christ

Forty fabulous days! More than a month elapsed between the resurrection of Christ and his ascension (Acts 1:3). During that time, he was on the earth in his resurrected body—that same body in which he had walked the dusty roads of Galilee and endured the torture of crucifixion on Calvary. That same body, alive again from the dead, and yet somehow gloriously transformed! He ate food in the presence of his disciples to prove that he was no disembodied spirit, no shadowy ghost, but himself, risen from the grave, as he had predicted. Yet he could appear and disappear at will, to the surprised group gathered behind closed doors or on the seashore.

After the ascension, he was not present in visible form, but only in spiritual presence, as the Holy Spirit, who is the Spirit of Christ, freed from all physical limitations, abiding with all true believers as the Paraclete, Comforter, Exhorter, Advocate. The question arises: Why that forty days interval? Why did the risen Lord not ascend to the Father immediately after his resurrection? His work was finished. He had suffered and died to pay the penalty for man's sins. Nothing could be added to that perfect life of complete obedience, offered to the heavenly Father on behalf of sinful humanity. Why then the delay in returning to his heavenly home, once his redemptive sacrifice had been accomplished?

A careful study of the four Gospels and the book of Acts provides the answer: Those forty days were no empty interlude. They were packed with exciting activity, as the risen Lord repeatedly appeared to his followers; carefully instructed them on the meaning of his life, his death, and his resurrection; and then told them what was expected of them as his witnesses, his representatives, on whom he depended for the continuation of all that he had begun to do and to teach (Acts 1:1). He could not leave it all to chance. He had to be sure that they understood and would carry out his instructions. So he appeared, explained the whole plan, and left it for them to consider. Then, about the time they began to doubt and wonder whether they had heard aright, he reappeared, went over it again, and reaffirmed his specific instructions to them. Not once, not twice, but at least three times and probably more, he appeared to large groups of his disciples, in addition to several appearances to individuals. Not only in Jerusalem, but also up in Galilee, where most of his disciples lived, he appeared, confirmed their faith, and renewed his instructions. By the end of the forty days, there was no room for reasonable doubt. They understood the plan. He had made it plain. He could now return to the Father, and leave the task to them, under the guidance and power of the Holy Spirit. For they had received and now they understood "The Great Commission!"

"The Great Commission" is a beautiful and meaningful phrase, but it has been much misunderstood. A common misconception is that Christ commanded his disciples to go into all the world and preach the gospel to all the nations only on one occasion. The various accounts in the Gospels and Acts are often telescoped and merged into one event. Indeed, the occasion is sometimes described as if the missionary commission had been almost an afterthought, hurriedly dictated just before the ascension, without any previous notice.

This is far from the truth! Not once, but again and again, the Lord explained his plans and laid upon his followers the responsibility of carrying them out. He delivered not so much "The Great Commission" as a series of great commissions, each with its distinctive emphasis, but all for a worldwide task!

Each of the four Gospels contains a statement of a missionary commission. In every case, it comes at the end of the book, as a fitting climax toward which the gospel narrative pointed. None of the Gospels tells the whole story. They supplement each other and are not complete without Luke's second account in the first chapter of the book of Acts. A synoptic view of the various appearances of the risen Lord and the instructions he gave to his disciples leaves no room for doubt concerning the importance he attached to the plan for witnessing to all the peoples of earth.

The Evening of the Resurrection Day

Mary Magdalene was the first to see the risen Christ (John 20:11-18), and soon afterward "the other women" saw him too (Matt. 28:5-10). Some time later that day, he appeared to Simon Peter (Luke 24:34). Then, late that evening two disciples from Emmaus recognized him as he broke bread in their home. We have already noted how they returned to Jerusalem and joined the group in the upper room, where the risen Lord appeared to all the disciples for the first time (Luke 24:36-49).

From this point, Luke and John give two different accounts of the words and actions of Jesus on that memorable night. Each complements the other, and both contain a missionary commission. Luke emphasizes the exposition of Old Testament Scriptures. As he had done on the road to Emmaus, Jesus quoted passages from the books of Moses, from the Prophets, and also from the Psalms, indicating that it was necessary for the Messiah to suffer, die, and rise again. From those same Scriptures, he showed that on the basis of his death and resurrection, repentance was now to be proclaimed in his name to all the nations, so that they might receive forgiveness for sins.

As previously indicated, that marvelous Bible class must have lasted an hour or more; the Scriptures quoted and interpreted were among those noted in the first three chapters of this book. Luke 24:46-47 constitutes a summary of the messianic teachings Jesus found in his Bible. It is important to notice that he not only emphasized the necessity of his suffering, death, and resurrection, but went on to make clear that the beneficiaries of his atoning death were to be "all the nations," and that the communicators of the good tidings were to be his disciples. A key verse is Luke 24:48: "You are witnesses of these things."[1]

The duty of a witness is to stand up and tell what he has seen, to testify concerning what he knows is truth. The statement "You are witnesses," both here and in Acts 1:8, is tantamount to a charge of responsibility to testify. It *is* a Great Commission! The disciples were warned not to attempt to witness in their own strength or wisdom, but to wait until they received the power of the Holy Spirit, which had been promised. Then, beginning in Jerusalem, they were to bear their witness, preach repentance, and proclaim the possibility of forgiveness and salvation *to all the nations.*

What a commission! Jesus said, "I have suffered, died, and risen again in fulfillment of the Scriptures. You are witnesses of these things. The Bible teaches that this message of salvation is intended for all the nations. Wait for the Holy Spirit to empower you. Then get to witnessing, and don't stop until all the peoples of earth have heard" (author's paraphrase).

John gives another account of this first meeting with the risen Christ. His summary in three verses is one of the shortest, but perhaps the most profound form of a Great Commission:

Jesus therefore said to them again, "Peace be with you; as the Father has sent Me, I also send you." And when He had said this, He breathed on them, and said to them, "Receive the Holy Spirit. If you forgive the sins of any, *their sins* have been forgiven them; if you retain the *sins* of any, they have been retained" (John 20:21-23).

"As the Father has sent Me, I also send you." What more compelling commission could be pronounced! Just as my Father sent me into the world to redeem the peoples of the world, so I am sending you into all the world as my representatives, the agents of the salvation which I have made possible. You know what a person must do to have his sins forgiven. He must repent of his sins and believe on me as his Lord and Savior. If you go and tell men how to be saved, some will repent and find that God has already forgiven them and provided for their salvation in the redeeming death of his Son. But if you do not tell them how to be saved, you leave them

with their sins unforgiven, because they have not repented and believed on me. It's up to you! I have done
all I can do. As the Father sent me, even so I send you!
Go, and tell the world how to be saved!

What a Great Commission!

The Second Appearance in Jerusalem

John tells us that the apostle Thomas was not present
at that first meeting in the upper room. When the other
disciples told him, "We have seen the Lord," Thomas
retorted, "I don't believe it! I won't believe it unless I
see the nail prints in his hands and actually put my fingers
into those prints and thrust my hand into that gaping
wound I saw in his side" (John 20:25, author's paraphrase).

"After eight days" is understood to mean "one week
later"; so it was probably the following Sunday evening
that Jesus appeared again to the disciples in the upper
room. This time Thomas was present. Jesus fixed his attention upon Thomas. He showed him his hands and
invited him to touch them and put his hand in the wound
on his side. But Thomas had seen enough! No further
proof was needed. He fell on his face in wonder, joy,
and adoration, exclaiming, "My Lord, and my God!"
(John 20:28).

The words of Jesus are a benediction to all succeeding
generations of believers: "Because you have seen me, you
have believed; blessed are they who have not seen and
yet have believed" (John 20:29, NIV).

John gives no further information about this second
encounter in Jerusalem. The emphasis was upon the need
for faith, with a rebuke to Thomas for his doubting spirit.
Mark's Gospel has preserved another account of a meet-

ing with the disciples. The time cannot be exactly pin-pointed, but there is evidence that it is the same meeting on the second Sunday night after the resurrection.

Mark 16:12-13 records the appearance to the two on the road to Emmaus, and states that they went and reported it to the other disciples, "but they did not believe them." We know from Luke and John that the disciples who saw the Lord that night did believe. So the reference must be to Thomas, and perhaps others who heard and did not believe the earliest reports of his appearance.

Mark 16:14 says, "Later Jesus appeared to the Eleven as they were eating; he rebuked them for their lack of faith and their stubborn refusal to believe those who had seen him after he had risen" (NIV). We are not told clearly how much later it was, but the conditions match those recorded by John concerning that second meeting. The eleven were present (including Thomas) and Jesus rebuked them for the unbelief. The words addressed to Thomas did apply to others to some degree, so that Mark's account is descriptive of the general tone of that meeting. But Mark tells what John failed to mention: After reproaching them for their lack of faith, Jesus explained again his plan for a worldwide mission: "Go into all the world and preach the good news to all creation. Whoever believes and is baptized will be saved, but whoever does not believe will be condemned" (Mark 16:15, NIV).

It is reasonable to believe that Jesus would not have confined his attention to Thomas, with no word for the others assembled on that occasion. They needed encouragement, not only to believe that he had risen from the dead, but that he meant what he had told them at the meeting a week earlier. After all, for a little band of Jewish believers, with all of their prejudices and the nationalistic hopes they had cherished, the instructions to mingle with Gentiles and inaugurate an international movement was too revolutionary to be received with immediate enthusiasm. Such a radical plan needed to be supported by the Scriptures, carefully explained, and repeated for emphasis. It was daring almost beyond belief! Luke and John tell us how the plan for worldwide witness was first presented. Mark almost certainly refers to the second presentation of a Great Commission the following week.

On a Mountain in Galilee

John tells of a third appearance to the disciples at the Sea of Tiberias, which was up in Galilee (John 21:1-18, note v. 14, "the third time"). No missionary commission is recorded, but the personal charge to Simon Peter, "Tend my sheep" and "Follow me," reflect the fact that these appearances were not just dramatic spectacles, but served as teaching sessions and left the disciples with a better understanding of the responsibility placed upon them.

Only Peter, Thomas, Nathaniel, James, and John, and two others were present at the lakeside (John 21:2). But a short time later, by special appointment, the eleven apostles gathered on a mountain in Galilee. Matthew 28:16-20 gives the best account. Paul's statement in 1 Corinthians 15:6 may refer to this same meeting. If so, more than five hundred brethren were present. If not, then Jesus appeared to this large company on some other occasion. Only in Galilee would that many of his followers be found, and at any such meeting the eleven would surely be included. It seems reasonable to conclude that Matthew and Paul are reporting the same event. Thus the words most commonly called "The Great Commission" were spoken, not to the apostles alone, but to a large group of disciples.

Matthew's account is probably a summary of a much longer statement, which may have included Scripture references to support the imperious claim of authority and the sweeping instructions for world evangelization. Even so, the brief command is startling in its comprehensiveness:

"All authority has been given to me." This must have been undergirded by references to the Messiah as God's chosen instrument for dealing with the nations.

"In heaven and on earth." These words echo Daniel 7:13-14, which pictures the Son of Man appearing before the Ancient of Days with the clouds of heaven, to be given dominion over all the peoples and nations of the earth.

"Go therefore." This is an accurate translation of the Greek text, used in most of the new versions. The verb form is not an imperative, but a participle. It can be translated literally, "Going" or "As you go." However, the main verb in the series, "make disciples," is an imperative, and as often in Greek usage, the accompanying participles carry the force of the principal verb. This is true of the words for "baptize" and "teach," both of which are participles, but have the force of a command. Here it is clear that the idea of going is not incidental or subordinate. The nations could not be "discipled" by persons remaining in Jerusalem. Going to where the people are is essential to the fulfillment of the commission. It is the clear command of our Lord.

"Make disciples of all the nations." The verb, *matheteusate,* is different from the word *teaching (didaskontes)* which follows. It means literally, "Enroll them in school as pupils"; "get them committed to my precepts"; "make them learners." While it includes the idea of teaching, the emphasis is upon the initial commitment, to be followed by detailed instruction. The word for "nations" is the same word often translated "Gentiles." The word for "all" occurs four times in these three verses: "*all* authority"; "*all* nations"; "*all* things I have commanded"; and "*all* the days." The comprehensiveness is intentional.

"Baptize them." The participle carries the force of a command. It is not optional, but an integral part of the commission.

"In the name of the Father and the Son and the Holy Spirit." The use of the Trinitarian formula has led some scholars to assume that this is a later interpretation of the Christian community, and not a direct quotation from Jesus himself. But he had instructed them concerning the coming of the Holy Spirit, and had repeatedly referred to God as Father and acknowledged before the high priest that he was the Son of God. Now in his glorified form he could clearly foresee the appropriate wording of their baptismal formula. Their impulse might be to baptize people in the name of Jesus, the Messiah. He wisely instructed them to make God the Father preeminent and not to forget the Holy Spirit, who would be so essential to the redemptive work. The fact that the word *name* is singular shows that the unity of the Godhead is assumed. Baptism was not to be in three different names, but in the name of the one God, who revealed himself in three personal aspects.

"Teaching them to observe all that I commanded you." Again the participle has the force of an imperative. The emphasis is not upon the content of the instruction so much as it is upon the *observance* of the commandments.

Obedience is the chief requirement. Accepting Jesus as Lord means enrolling in his school, becoming a disciple or learner, and then obeying his teachings as they are progressively received, all of which will have the force of commandments, because of his inherent authority.

"I am with you always, even to the end of the age." The promise of his presence is guaranteed by his authoritarian position as an eternal king, whose dominion is worldwide in extent and timeless in its duration. A literal translation is: "And behold, I am with you all the days until the completion of the aeon."

This imperious pronouncement is either the grandiose boast of a deluded egotist, or it is the clear, reasonable delineation of a plan by which the eternal God has decided to deal with the entire human race through his anointed Messiah and those who accept him as King of kings and Lord of lords. Which do you think it is?

The Final Commission

Matthew's Gospel ends abruptly after the Great Commission, the climax toward which the whole narrative pointed. This has led some to assume that the statement recorded by Matthew was the final commission before the ascension. But that is clearly not the case. Matthew's account is of a meeting on a mountain in Galilee, many miles from Bethany, the scene of the ascension. There was plenty of time for the apostles, who had gone back to their homes in Galilee after the Passover, to return to Jerusalem for the final appearance on the Mount of Olives, near Bethany. Forty days had elapsed since the resurrection. The two appearances at Jerusalem had been followed by at least two appearances in Galilee, one by the Sea of Tiberias, the other on a hilltop. There had been a personal appearance to James, the half brother of Jesus (1 Cor. 15:7), and perhaps other appearances not recorded in the Gospels. Jesus was now satisfied that the apostles and other disciples understood the meaning of his death and the universal scope of his kingdom, now established, but yet to be extended both geographically and to future generations. Even so, he reviewed the plan and repeated the commission one more time just prior to his departure. Dr. Luke, the author of the book of Acts, gives us the account in Acts 1:1-12.

It is usually assumed that only the eleven apostles witnessed the ascension and heard the last missionary commission. The eleven are listed by name in Acts 1:13, and Paul's reference in 1 Corinthians 15:7 seems to support the view that they alone were present. But there is evidence that others shared that tremendous experience. The apostles were part of a group of about 120 which met continually for prayer in the upper room (Acts 1:14-15). When the time came to choose someone to take the place of Judas Iscariot, two men were put forward, Joseph Barsabbas and Matthias (Acts 1:23). They both had the necessary qualifications: namely, that they had accompanied the apostles all through the ministry of Jesus, "beginning with the baptism of John, until the day he was taken up from us" (Acts 1:22). This strongly implies that these two men were eyewitnesses of the ascension. And if they were there, it may well be that others were also, including "the women" (probably wives of the apostles) and Mary, the mother of Jesus, and his brothers, all of whom are mentioned as belonging to the group meeting regularly in the upper room. So the last of "the Great Commissions" may have been delivered to a much larger group than the eleven apostles. In any case, it did not apply exclusively to them, and they at once involved others, both men and women, in prayerful preparation for the coming of the Spirit.

Whatever the number, the group gathered on the Mount of Olives was not very perceptive. Despite the fact that Jesus had presented himself to them over a period of forty days, "speaking of the things concerning the kingdom of God (Acts 1:3), they still could not quite grasp the idea of a worldwide spiritual kingdom. They were obsessed with the concept of a reestablished Jewish nation, free from Roman rule. If Jesus had not accomplished this during his normal life, perhaps he would now bring it about by some miraculous apocalyptic event. After his resurrection, they were ready to believe almost any miracle. Hence the naive question: "Lord, are you at this time going to restore the kingdom of Israel?" (Acts 1:6, NIV).

Annoyance and rebuke are easy to detect in the reply of Jesus: "That's none of your business!" would be a good paraphrase of his words. "Don't ask questions about time schedules or epochs, which will be determined by the heavenly Father without consulting you! You have only one concern: you are to receive power when the Holy Spirit has come upon you; and you shall then be my witnesses, both in Jerusalem, and in all Judea and Samaria, and even to the remotest part of the earth" (Acts 1:7-8, author's paraphrase).

Once again, the worldwide scope of the Kingdom is emphasized, and the witnessing role of the disciples is clear. The essential work of the Holy Spirit is inescapable. More than in the other commissions, the geographical concept is dominant, with orderly progress from the home base, out into neighboring territories, and ultimately to

the ends of the earth. It could not all be accomplished
at once. Nor could they do anything in their own strength.
They were to wait for the coming of the Holy Spirit,
and then, under his power and guidance, begin where
they were, bear witness to what they had seen and heard,
to the Jews first, of course, then to the Samaritans, and
on to the Gentile nations at the ends of the earth.

This was not something new to the apostles. They had
heard it on the evening of the resurrection day; then
again one week later. It had been impressively explained
to them on the mountain in Galilee. And now, by way
of review, it was underscored for the last time. There
was no room for doubt in their minds as to the intention
of Jesus. He had heard his Father say, "Ask of Me, and
I will surely give the nations as Thy inheritance, and
the *very* ends of the earth as Thy possession" (Ps. 2:8),
even as the inspired psalmist had foreseen. "And to Him
was given dominion, Glory and a kingdom, That all
the peoples, nations, and *men of every* language might serve
Him," just as the prophet Daniel had predicted (Dan.
7:14). By suffering, he had entered into his glory, and
now, just as the Father had sent him, he, with the authority given to him, was sending his faithful followers and
witnesses out to make real his claim to an everlasting
dominion "from sea to sea, and from the River to the
ends of the earth," which Zechariah had said would be
his (Zech. 9:10).

The Great Commission is not an incidental statement
to be shrugged off by skeptical or uncommitted disciples,
either in the first century or the twentieth. It is the master
plan of the Messiah, based upon numerous Scriptures,
and made effective by his death and resurrection. Knowing that his Kingdom was not of this world, he disdained

to be enthroned by zealous Zionistic revolutionaries, who wanted to throw off the despised Gentile rule of Rome and restore the Davidic line. Convinced that he, if lifted up on the cross, would draw all men to himself (John 12:32), he had set his face steadfastly toward Jerusalem, knowing that suffering and death awaited him, but equally certain that the Father would raise him up and give him glory and a Kingdom without end. He had tried to explain it before his death, but the disciples could not understand and did not really believe him. Now, vindicated by his resurrection, he interpreted the Scriptures again, and for the first time they began to grasp the truth and see the glorious nature of the Kingdom which the Lord had prepared for them. Patiently he went over it each time he appeared to them, knowing full well that their prejudices would hinder them and the magnitude of the task would discourage them, but he must depend upon them to carry on what he had begun.

They got the message! So much so that each Gospel writer made it the climax of his story: Matthew, Mark, Luke, and John, all build up to the "punch line"—a Great Commission! And Luke, in his second discourse, the book of Acts, begins with another commission and shows that what followed in the next thirty years was the logical outgrowth of the risen Lord's clear instructions. Not with monotonous sameness, but with rich variety, the plan is reiterated five times in the New Testament—the "Great Commissions," they may be called. But the singular is better, so long as the richness, the variety, and the greatness are understood: it is "The Great Commission," the master plan of the Messiah; grounded in the Scriptures; made possible by his suffering and atoning death; repeatedly communicated to his disciples, as binding upon all succeeding generations of believers; to be effectuated by the power and guidance of the Holy Spirit. For God so loved the world—the whole world—that he gave his only begotten son, that whosoever—of whatever race, language, or tribe—believes on him, might not perish, but have eternal life!

Note

1. This may be an indirect reference to Isaiah 43:10,12 and 44:8: "You are my witnesses." What Israel had failed to do, the New Israel is now commissioned to fulfill.

VII.
Acts: First Chapter in Mission History

Concern for "All Nations" looms large in the book of Acts. The author was probably a Gentile—Luke, "the beloved physician," who also wrote the Gospel which bears his name. He accompanied Paul on many of his travels, and as a Gentile convert had a special interest in the spread of the faith and the incorporation of various racial groups within the new "People of God." But he was even more concerned to explain how the Christian religion won victory after victory over persons and practices which would have hindered its progress toward becoming "the faith of all mankind."

The appropriateness of the title, "The Acts of the Apostles," has often been questioned, but the fault lies largely in the translation of the terse Greek title, *Praxeis Apostolon*. There is no article before the word for "acts" or "of apostles." Since the word *apostle* means "one sent forth," or "missionary," a good translation would be "Doings of Missionaries," or "Deeds of Those Sent Out." Luke obviously makes no effort to record all the activities of the twelve apostles. He does recount some of the activities of some missionaries who were responsible for the early spread of Christianity. In this sense, the book can be considered the first chapter in the history of Christian missions.

Without Luke's account, it would be hard to understand how Christianity, which began in Jerusalem as a movement within Judaism, within about thirty-five years had spread to nearly all parts of the Roman Empire and was rapidly becoming a Gentile religion, repudiated and bitterly opposed by most Jews. This was exactly what Luke undertook to explain to Theophilus, to whom his treatise was dedicated (Acts 1:1).

At the time Luke wrote, his dear friend Paul was in prison, awaiting trial on charges brought against him by Jewish leaders in Jerusalem. The exact nature of the charges is not clear (Acts 24:5-6; 25:18-21). The basic complaint seems to have been that Paul had departed from the Jewish faith and was teaching heresies which amounted to a dangerous new sect. He therefore was not entitled to protection under Roman law, which recognized Judaism, but vigorously suppressed illicit religions. Paul's defense was that he was a staunch and faithful Jew, and that all his teachings were based upon Old Testament Scriptures which Jesus, his Lord, had fulfilled, just as many Hebrew prophets had predicted.

Luke's treatise may have been designed as a lawyer's brief for use at Paul's trial, as some have theorized.[1] But it was far more than that. It was an inspired testimony that the Jesus way was not some strange new sect spreading dangerous doctrines, but was the true fulfillment of Judaism, vindicated by miraculous evidences of God's favor, widely accepted by persons of many different races, and destined to become the religion of all mankind.

To achieve this purpose, Luke traced the geographical spread of Christianity from Jerusalem to Rome, taking note of its numerical growth at various stages. He gave special attention to the inclusion of new ethnic groups within the growing Christian community, and in the process revealed the reasons for Jewish criticism and opposition. He made it clear that this way was by divine plan designed for all nations, and that the Jews had not been excluded, but had voluntarily and deliberately excluded themselves, preferring their own narrow, nationalistic traditions above the free and open international fellowship to be found in the Christian community.

Many elements are skillfully woven together in this exciting account of the first phase of Christian development. Let us note some of the points Doctor Luke makes as he moves confidently toward a triumphant conclusion.

1 Geographical Expansion

Luke begins the book of Acts right where he left off in his Gospel. He had told how the risen Christ appeared in the upper room on the evening of the resurrection day and explained from the Scriptures why it was necessary for him to die, and how on the basis of his death and resurrection repentance and forgiveness of sin was to be preached to all nations (Luke 24:44-49). Skipping quickly over the forty days that followed, he comes to the last appearance on the Mount of Olives just before the ascension. Note carefully what Jesus said in that last commission: "But you shall receive power when the Holy Spirit has come upon you; and you shall be My witnesses both in Jerusalem, and in all Judea and Samaria, and even to the remotest part of the earth" (Acts 1:8).

Luke then proceeds to tell how the disciples obeyed that last command. It is almost as though the words of Christ formed an outline in the mind of Luke, and consciously or unconsciously he follows that outline in the broad framework of his book. The story unfolds just as Jesus said it would.

Chapters 1 and 2 tell how the Holy Spirit came on the day of Pentecost and how the disciples began witnessing with power and effectiveness. Chapters 3 through 7 describe witnessing activities in and around Jerusalem. At chapter 8 the scene changes because of persecution in Jerusalem, and the disciples were "scattered throughout the regions of Judea and Samaria" (Acts 8:1). Wherever they went, they witnessed. Luke gives special attention to events in Samaria and in Damascus, the capital of Syria, but still on the outskirts of Judea-Samaria.

At chapter 13 there is a definite widening of the area of witnessing, as Barnabas and Paul set out from Antioch of Syria on a sea voyage westward. The gospel is now on its way toward "the uttermost parts of the earth," and there is to be no stopping it! The third phase of the Great Commission has begun, under the guidance and power of the Holy Spirit, just as Jesus said it would!

Luke makes no pretense of telling all that happened in the early spread of the gospel. His main emphasis is upon the journeys of Paul and his companions. From chapter 16 onward, much that he relates is as an eyewitness and participant. He tells what he knows about geographical extension, but recognizes that the gospel reached some places before he and Paul got there. This was true of the city of Rome. With amazing accuracy and keen attention to detail, Luke names districts and cities into which Christianity penetrated: Cyprus, Cilicia, Lycaonia, Galatia, Macedonia, and Achaia; Philippi, Thessalonica, Athens, Corinth, Ephesus, and Rome. His book reads almost like a geographical gazette! And there is a certain sense of completeness and finality when at last he describes his favorite missionary, Paul, freely witnessing to all who come to him in the capital of the greatest empire on earth at that time! All of this happened, Luke explains, in obedience to the clear instructions of the risen Christ, in fulfillment of Scriptures, and by the power and guidance of the Holy Spirit, whom he had promised!

2 Numerical Growth

But geographical expansion is not all. Luke is interested in numbers! His scientific mind seems to be fascinated with geometrical increase, and he glories in the significance of statistical growth. He takes pains to point out that the twelve had increased to 120 even before the coming of the Holy Spirit (Acts 1:15). He rejoices in the 3,000 souls added to the church by baptism on the day of Pentecost (Acts 2:41), and reports that soon afterward about 5,000 men were believers, to say nothing of the women and children (Acts 4:4). After that he makes no attempt to give definite figures, but periodically reports the continuing growth of the church. At six points in his book, he pauses to summarize the situation. Each summary marks the end of one phase of Kingdom expansion. Each time it is possible to record dynamic growth.

Acts 6:7 is the first such summary. It follows the account of the choosing of seven men to assist in distributing relief to widows and other needy persons in the Jerusalem congregation. All the witnessing up to this point had been in the city of Jerusalem. Luke is about to tell how the bold preaching of Stephen, one of the seven, led to his martyrdom and to the scattering of the disciples throughout Judea and Samaria. His confident summary emphasizes three things: geographical spread, numerical growth, and the winning of converts from one of the most resistant elements of the population, the priesthood. Luke says: "And the word of God kept on spreading; and the number of the disciples continued to increase greatly in Jerusalem, and a great many of the priests were becoming obedient to the faith."

Acts 9:31 summarizes the situation a few years later. No longer is the church confined to Jerusalem. Philip has witnessed in Samaria and the results have been confirmed by Peter and John. The Ethiopian eunuch has been sent on his way rejoicing, and Philip has preached in all the cities from Azotus to Caesarea. Saul, on his way to arrest believers in Damascus, up in Syria, has experienced a miraculous conversion. Most of the converts have been either Jews or Samaritans, with few Gentiles among them. Luke is about to tell how the first Romans were won in the household of Cornelius. He looks back upon the period just closing with this optimistic observation: "So the church throughout all Judea and Galilee and Samaria enjoyed peace, being built up; and, going on in the fear of the Lord and in the comfort of the Holy Spirit, it continued to increase."

Acts 12:24 is one of the briefest of Luke's summaries. It follows his account of Peter's mission to Caesarea and his subsequent imprisonment by Herod. Luke is now ready to tell how Paul and Barnabas were sent out by the church at Antioch, inaugurating the first planned mission beyond Judea, Samaria, and the neighboring territory of Syria. He puts it succinctly: "But the word of the Lord continued to grow and to be multiplied." Then he goes on to the next phase of expansion.

Acts 16:5 is Luke's short summary of the situation just

before he joined Paul and Silas on their historic mission to Macedonia, crossing from the continent of Asia to Europe. He modestly refrains from any personal reference, except the use of the personal pronouns, "we" and "us," used for the first time at Acts 16:10, indicating that the author has now become involved. Conscious that the next stage of expansion is epochal in its significance, and still concerned with numerical growth, Luke gives a final touch to the period just closed, involving the churches of Asia Minor: "So the churches were being strengthened in the faith, and were increasing in number daily."

Acts 19:20 is another terse summary, coming just after Paul's third journey, as the apostle resolves to return to Jerusalem. All that God had done through Paul and other faithful witnesses is put in these words: "So the word of the Lord was growing mightily and prevailing."

Luke's final summary comes at the end of the book, Acts 28:30-31, as Paul, now in Rome at last, after many adventures, symbolizes the remarkable growth that has taken place, and the freedom and opportunity which are now available to the growing Christian forces: "And he stayed two full years in his own rented quarters, and was welcoming all who came to him, preaching the kingdom of God, and teaching concerning the Lord Jesus Christ with all openness, unhindered."

Crossing Racial Barriers

But Luke's interest is not confined to geographical expansion and numerical growth. He also shows a keen concern for the racial or ethnic factor. Himself a Gentile, he is concerned to recount how the Christian faith, beginning as a sect of Judaism, has by the year A.D. 64 become identified more with Gentiles than with Jews; indeed, is finding its most determined opposition from the ranks of respectable Jewish communities, who seem eager to disassociate themselves from the vigorous new movement, and who sometimes stir up persecution by the Roman authorities. His book has been regarded by some as an apologetic treatise, compiled as a defense against the charge that Christians are troublemakers who have no right to pose as Jews and thus claim protection under Roman law, which recognized Judaism as an officially approved religion.

Whatever his motive, Luke gives careful attention to each instance in which a new racial group is reached by the gospel, convinced that it is the purpose of God, revealed in Old Testament Scriptures, to take for himself a special people, redeemed by the Messiah's suffering and death, to form a New Israel, an international people, from among all the nations of earth.

Not one of the twelve apostles, but one of the first deacons became the pioneer in proclaiming Christ to persons who were not Jews. Philip preached first to the Samaritans and then to the Ethiopian eunuch. We are told that it was under the guidance of the Holy Spirit that he witnessed to the Ethiopian (Acts 8:29). While no mention is made of the Spirit's direction that he should go to Samaria, it is strongly implied, and we are told that Philip performed signs and miracles in Samaria, and that he baptized converts in the name of Jesus Christ even before the arrival of Peter and John. The apostles had been too busy preaching and baptizing in Jerusalem to go on a mission to Samaria. But when news came of the conversion of Samaritans, it occasioned no great surprise, and at once two apostles were sent to confirm the work of Philip. There is little doubt that the early Christians regarded the twelve apostles as having some type of spiritual authority, and it is significant that the gift of the Holy Spirit was not received until Peter and John prayed for them and laid hands on them. This insured that the inclusion of Samaritans within the Christian community had official approval of the apostles, who had been appointed by the Lord himself, who had made it clear that his mission was not confined to Israel. While it would not be possible for the twelve personally to validate each new racial group to be received into the growing church, policies and principles were being established, and care was taken to preserve the unity of the new movement.

Philip baptized the Ethiopian without specific authorization from the apostles or the Jerusalem church. There is no evidence that an apostolic delegation followed the eunuch as he returned to his native land, rejoicing in his newfound faith. Neither is there any reason to believe that Philip's action came under the criticism of the apostles. The baptism of the Ethiopian seems to have been accepted as a proper thing to do, in view of the commission which the risen Lord had given, and the impulse of the Holy Spirit, which had been so clear to Philip. Obviously, there were no practical problems of relationship to the Jerusalem community, since Ethiopia was so far away.

Samaritans and an Ethiopian were received without too much difficulty. The reception of the first Roman convert called for special attention, partly because Cornelius was a despised Gentile military man in command of the Roman army of occupation, and partly because Caesarea was not very far from Jerusalem.

In spite of the example of Jesus during his ministry and the clear instructions given after his resurrection, it was no easy thing for Peter to go into the home of a Gentile, thus incurring ceremonial defilement. To preach repentance and forgiveness of sins to a Roman military officer was for Simon Peter similar to the call for Jonah to preach to the people of Nineveh. Peter's first reaction might have been the same as Jonah's, but for the heavenly vision, thrice repeated, which prepared him to respond to the request that he visit the home of Cornelius (Acts 10:10-16). Surprised as he was at the Lord's command for him to eat food which he had considered "unclean," he at once saw the parallel when the Spirit instructed him to go to a Gentile home, which he likewise considered "unclean." To Cornelius and his household Peter put it quite bluntly: "You yourselves know how unlawful it is for a man who is a Jew to associate with a foreigner or to visit him; and yet God has shown me that I should not call any man unholy or unclean. That is why I came without even raising any objection when I was sent for" (Acts 10:28).

Luke is careful to point out that the Holy Spirit fell upon all who were listening to Peter's message before he even finished his sermon—"while [he] was still speaking these words" (Acts 10:44). He had planned to say more, but it was not necessary. Peter had explained how Jesus died, rose from the grave and ordered his witnesses to testify "that this is the One who has been appointed by God as Judge of the living and the dead" (Acts 10:42). He then added: "Of Him all the prophets bear witness that through His name every one who believes in Him has received forgiveness of sins" (Acts 10:43). That was enough! "Everyone who believes in Him!"

The expression used by Simon Peter is as broad and inclusive as the Greek language can make it. "Whosoever" is the translation in the King James Version. There is no limitation of race, culture, or nationality. The sole condition is faith: "Whosoever believeth." Cornelius and his family had been listening eagerly, wondering whether they could receive forgiveness of sins. The moment Peter stated the condition for salvation, they met that condition: they believed in Jesus, the crucified, risen Messiah, as Judge of the living and the dead. At that instant they experienced the joy of salvation and began praising God, as the Holy Spirit gave them utterance. The evidences of the presence and power of the Holy Spirit in their lives were so obvious that Peter arranged at once for their baptism.

Small wonder that Peter had to explain his actions upon his return to Jerusalem; and how glad he was that he had taken witnesses with him, who could confirm that God had done it, not Peter. There could be only one answer to Peter's question, "If God therefore gave them the same gift as He *gave* to us also after believing in the Lord Jesus Christ, who was I that I could stand in God's way?" (Acts 11:17). Even those who had raised the objections quieted down and joined in praising God, saying, "Well then, God has granted to the Gentiles also the repentance *that leads* to life" (v. 18).

It might be expected that the conversion of Cornelius and the evidence that this had divine approval would have resulted in widespread witnessing to Gentiles. But Luke makes it clear that, even after this remarkable occurrence, the general practice of the believers as they traveled about was to bear witness only to Jews. The practice of the group in Antioch was an exception to the rule.

They began "speaking to the Greeks also, preaching the Lord Jesus" (Acts 11:20). We are not told that the Greek converts received the gift of the Spirit in a miraculous way, giving visible evidence that God had placed his seal upon them as members of the new people of God. But this is strongly implied in the words, "and the hand of the Lord was with them," and the statement that Barnabas, who was sent to investigate the situation, "witnessed the grace of God," and was satisfied with what he saw (vv. 21,23). He apparently reported to the church at Jerusalem that the inclusion of Greeks within the church at Antioch was the work of the Holy Spirit, not to be questioned.

Luke took notice of the first Samaritans, the first Romans, and the first Greeks to be received into the Christian fellowship, as examples of the way the movement was widening. From Acts 13, with the departure of Paul and Barnabas on their first missionary journey, Luke begins to use the general term, "the Gentiles," to denote the non-Jewish groups that were brought in. It was not possible to specify each separate racial type that was touched by the Gospel. Mention is made of the Lycaonians at Lystra (Acts 14:11), and the "barbarians" on the island of Malta (Acts 28:2-4). But Luke reverts to the expression "both Jews and Greeks" repeatedly, using "Greeks" as a synonym for "Gentiles" (Acts 14:1; 18:4; 19:10,17). His point has been made. Non-Jewish believers of whatever race or background were consistently received into the church when they believed and repented of their sins. By the end of the book of Acts, about A.D. 64, Gentile Christians probably outnumbered Jewish believers.

Overcoming Tradition and Ritualism

Even more important than geographical expansion, numerical growth, or even the inclusion of new racial groups, was the struggle of the Christian movement for spiritual freedom: the recognition that salvation was by grace through faith, not of works; and that the believer did not need to repudiate his own culture and nationality in order to be saved. This was the most troublesome issue. It involved theological controversy within the church itself.

Many of the early Jewish converts who accepted Jesus as the promised Messiah were faithful Pharisees. Like Saul of Tarsus, they had lived according to the strictest sect of Judaism. It was difficult for them to conceive that a person could be saved without conforming to all the Jewish ceremonial requirements which they had taught so thoroughly; there soon developed within the new Christian movement a group commonly called "Judaizers," who insisted that Gentiles who accepted Jesus as Messiah must also accept circumcision and the dietary laws which were binding on all faithful Jews. They did not say that Gentiles could not be received. The teachings of Jesus on this point were too clear to be denied. But they wanted to specify conditions for receiving Gentile converts which would have been similar to those for receiving proselytes into the Jewish community. To baptism, which was required of proselytes, and which Jesus commanded, they would have added circumcision, about which Jesus said nothing. The issue was not really race, but ritual. It involved not a spiritual state, but a physical condition.

4

Accepting a Eunuch

The first instance of relaxing the rigid pharisaical rules for receiving converts into the Kingdom is often overlooked. It was the Ethiopian eunuch. He was not only non-Jewish in his racial origin; he was a member of a category of persons who had been barred from fellowship and worship in the Temple by reason of a physical handicap. As a eunuch, he was not a normal male specimen. According to Deuteronomy 23:1, no eunuch was permitted to enter "the assembly of the Lord." This ruling had been enforced during much of Hebrew history. But Isaiah had foretold a time when eunuchs, as well as foreigners, would be permitted to enter the house of the Lord, if they kept the sabbath and observed the covenant (Isa. 56:3-5). This is the same passage to which Jesus referred at the time of the cleansing of the Temple (Mark 11:17). He must have felt that he would bring about the fulfillment of Isaiah's prophecy concerning eunuchs, even as he opened the way for aliens to come to the Lord. On another occasion, Jesus made a statement which indicated that, far from excluding one, being a eunuch might even help a person to enter the kingdom of heaven.[2] The spirit of Jesus was the inspiration of Paul's later declaration that in Christ "there is neither Jew nor Greek, there is neither slave nor free man, there is neither male nor female" (Gal. 3:28). No external physical condition is a factor. Each individual is accepted as a person. Faith in Christ is the only requirement.

Philip had received this insight from the Spirit, who directed him to preach to the Ethiopian. When the eunuch saw a stream of water and asked, "Why can't I be baptized?" Philip's ready answer was, "Of course you may, if you believe."[3] Faith was the only requirement. After his baptism, the eunuch went on his way rejoicing, not only that he had found Christ as his Savior, but because he had been accepted as a person, without reference to his physical handicap.

The Question of Circumcision

Since the eunuch returned to Ethiopia, no questions were raised about his baptism. Ethiopia was far from Jerusalem and there was no possibility of socializing with the eunuch. The baptism of uncircumcised Gentile believers posed a different problem since they often lived in the midst of a Jewish community. The church had to decide whether Jewish Christians could mingle freely with Gentile converts without defiling themselves, and whether Gentiles could have the assurance of salvation without going all the way required of proselytes to Judaism. The issue became acute after Paul and Barnabas returned from their missionary journey through Asia Minor and reported to the church at Antioch how God had "opened a door of faith to the Gentiles" (Acts 14:27). Soon afterward some men came down from Judea and began teaching the brethren, "Unless you are circumcised according to the custom of Moses, you cannot be saved" (Acts 15:1).

Paul and Barnabas disagreed with the "Judaizers" and argued strongly that Gentile converts should not be required to meet these ritualistic regulations. In order to avoid a rupture in the fellowship, the Antioch church decided to send Paul and Barnabas to Jerusalem to confer with the apostles and elders of the mother church about this issue. Acts 15 gives an account of the conference that was held. Apparently the Jerusalem congregation first heard the report of Paul and Barnabas, but when the Judaizers hotly challenged the practice of receiving Gentile converts without requiring the men to be circumcised, the meeting was adjourned and the apostles and elders met in executive session to consider the matter (Acts 15:6). After full discussion, a decision was reached, and the committee reported back to the full congregation, which agreed that the Gentile believers would be welcomed into the Christian fellowship with no further ceremonial requirement, except that they abstain from food offered to idols, and from meat of animals killed by strangulation, so that the blood was not drained from the carcass. This was to avoid offense to Jews who believed that "the life is in the blood," and were repelled by the manner in which Gentiles sometimes slaughtered animals. The believers were also admonished to abstain from fornication, so often prevalent among pagans (compare Acts 15:20; 15:29). But significantly, they were not required to be circumcised or to eat only "kosher" foods, as would have been expected of full proselytes to Judaism.

In presenting the matter to the Jerusalem church, Peter made a significant statement: "We believe that we are saved through the grace of the Lord Jesus, in the same way as they also are" (Acts 15:11). "We" here means "we Jews who have believed in Jesus as the Messiah." Peter did not say, "We believe that the Gentiles are saved by grace through faith, just as we Jews have been." It was obvious that the Gentiles had been saved by faith alone, since they had done nothing to receive the gift of the Holy Spirit and the joyful experience of forgiveness, except to believe on Jesus Christ. By observing how Gentiles had been saved, the Jewish Christians were better able to understand how they themselves were saved. The indispensable factor in both cases was faith. Jewish believers realized that they had not been saved by circumcision nor by any works of the Law, but "by the grace of the Lord Jesus," just as in the case of Gentile converts.

The decision of the Jerusalem conference was a significant victory for the universality of the gospel. It established the fact that a person of any nationality could come into the Christian fellowship without renouncing his own cultural heritage and becoming a Jewish proselyte. Jesus had noted the tendency for converts to Pharisaism to become more rigid in their beliefs and practices than natural-born Jews. "Woe unto you, scribes and Pharisees, hypocrites," he had declared, "because you travel about on sea and land to make one proselyte; and when he becomes one, you make him twice as much a son of hell as yourselves" (Matt. 23:15). Anyone who would consent to repudiate his own race and nationality by submitting to circumcision and accepting the full round of pharisaic legal and ritualistic requirements would necessarily become quite legalistic, placing undue emphasis upon external conformity, and missing the joy and freedom which come from genuine forgiveness and fellowship with God and his people.

This would have been the result if Gentile converts had been required to become full Jewish proselytes, accepting circumcision and the ritual and dietary laws. Furthermore, many Gentiles would have declined to identify themselves with the Christian movement if these conditions had been recognized and enforced. The spiritual victory won at Jerusalem insured that the gospel would continue to have free access to the Gentiles, and that multitudes would respond with joy to the invitation to accept Jesus as Messiah and Savior, on the basis of salvation by grace through faith, not of works, either moral or ritualistic.

The Self-Exclusion of the Jews

Luke has shown much of the geographical spread of Christianity and its numerical growth. With the conclusion of Acts 15, the universal appeal of the gospel has been established: Gentiles are free to enter the Kingdom without becoming Jewish proselytes. The conversion of the Philippian jailer and his household, recorded in chapter 16, marks another epoch, in that this was the first instance in which pagans who had no previous knowledge of Judaism were converted. Apparently up to this point Gentile converts had been "God-fearers," sympathetic students of Judaism, but not full proselytes. But the Philippian jailer was from a heathen background, with little or no knowledge of the God of Israel. With his baptism, as Frank Stagg has observed, "The last group had now been reached."[4]

But Luke had an additional purpose in writing the book of Acts, and to this much of the latter half of the book is directed. He must show, not only how Gentiles in large numbers came within the new Christian movement, but how the Jews typically rejected the teaching that Jesus was their longed-for Messiah, leaving the movement by about A.D. 64 dominantly Gentile in its constituency. Luke is careful to point out that this was a deliberate choice on the part of the majority of the Jews. They had not been neglected in the preaching of the good news. They had not been rejected by God or excluded by the Gentile members. It was clearly a matter of their own "self-exclusion."[5]

Paul and his companions habitually went to the synagogue upon arriving in a new city. There he preached to Jews and "God-fearers," Gentiles who were interested in Judaism, but had not yet become full proselytes. On his first journey, Jewish opposition caused Paul and Barnabas at Pisidian Antioch to declare: "It was necessary that the word of God should be spoken to you first; since you repudiate it, and judge yourselves unworthy of eternal life, behold, we are turning to the Gentiles" (Acts 13:46). This meant only that in that city they ceased trying to meet in the synagogue. But at the next city, Iconium, they began meetings in the synagogue and continued until persecution forced them to flee (Acts 14:-1-5).

On the second missionary journey, accompanied by Silas, Paul once again went to the synagogue, "according to his custom," at Thessalonica (Acts 17:1), at Berea (Acts 17:10), and at Corinth (Acts 18:1). Indeed, at Corinth, he seems to have concentrated his efforts on winning Jewish believers, after the arrival of Silas and Timothy allowed him to give up tentmaking and devote his full time to expounding the Scriptures. Whereas before "he was reasoning in the synagogue every Sabbath and trying to persuade Jews and Greeks," he now began "devoting himself completely to the word, solemnly testifying to the Jews that Jesus was the Christ (the Messiah)" (Acts 18:4-5).

It was only when the Jews at Corinth stubbornly resisted his teaching that Paul finally shook out his garments in symbolic indignation, saying, "Your blood *be* upon your own heads! I am clean; [I have no further responsibility for your fate.] from now on I shall go to the Gentiles" (Acts 18:6).

This meant only that Paul would quit striving in vain to persuade the Jews in Corinth. When he left there and went to Ephesus, once again "he himself entered the synagogue and reasoned with the Jews" (Acts 18:19). On a second visit to Ephesus, he continued meeting in the synagogue for three months before the opposition became so sharp that he withdrew and began teaching daily in the school of Tyrannus, probably a public hall for lectures and other meetings. There he continued for two years. The break with the synagogue seems to have been complete; not because Paul was forced to leave, nor because of any lack of concern for his kinsmen, but because he wished to reach both Jews and Greeks without constant friction and opposition (Acts 19:8-10).[6]

Although Paul was constrained again and again in turn from the resistant Jews to the more responsive Gentiles, he never completely abandoned his own people and nation. He was convinced that God's plan was "to the Jew first, and also to the Gentile." Distressed at the widening gulf between the synagogue and the church, he resolved to make one last effort to preserve the unity of the Christian movement. This involved a return to Jerusalem for another conference with the elders of "the Mother Church," and a determined attempt to testify that Jesus was the Messiah at the very spot where he had first been rejected.

Seemingly Paul clung to the hope that his message might be accepted in Jerusalem, until a riot in the Temple and the exposed plot of the chief priests and official leaders made it clear that the Jews as a whole would not recognize Jesus as the Messiah. To save his own life, reluctantly Paul appealed to Caesar. This symbolized his identification with the Gentile world as over against the

Jewish nation. Paul chose Rome instead of Jerusalem. But only when Jerusalem and the Jewish nation decisively rejected his message, which was exactly the same message that the risen Christ had expounded to his disciples: That it was necessary for the Messiah to suffer, die, and rise again from the dead on the third day, according to the Scriptures; and that repentance and the forgiveness of sins was to be proclaimed in his name to all the nations, beginning at Jerusalem.

The Jews had the first opportunity to accept their Messiah and recognize him as Lord of all the nations and Savior of all mankind. Many did believe, but progressively, as more and more Gentiles rejoiced to learn that they were included in God's plan of redemption, the Jews hardened their hearts, refusing to believe that the Messiah was to be "A LIGHT OF REVELATION TO THE GENTILES," as well as "the glory of Thy people Israel" (Luke 2:32, based on Isa. 42:6; 49:6).

The book of Acts closes with Paul in Rome, capital of the greatest empire of that day. In custody awaiting trial on charges brought against him by the Jews of Jerusalem, he was allowed to stay in his own rented quarters and to receive visitors. The first group invited were "the leading men of the Jews" (Acts 28:17), who came in large numbers to hear Paul testify about the Kingdom of God and try to persuade them that Jesus was the Messiah, "both from the Law of Moses and from the Prophets" (Acts 28:23), from morning until evening. Once again, some believed, but others would not. Paul, after quoting an appropriate passage from Isaiah 6:9-10 concerning their hardness of heart, declared with a certain finality, "Let it be known to you therefore, that this salvation of God has been sent to the Gentiles. They will listen [even though you will not]" (Acts 28:28).

Luke's task is now complete. He has shown how the good news was proclaimed, in obedience to the command of the risen Lord, in Jerusalem, then throughout all Judea and Samaria, and out to the uttermost parts of the earth. He has described its numerical growth as it became a significant factor in the religious life of the Greco-Roman Empire. He has noted how it crossed racial and cultural barriers, becoming truly international in its constituency. He has recorded sadly how the Jews have typically excluded themselves from the growing Christian community, leaving it largely a Gentile movement.

His treatise ends with an unusual adverb, which may be translated "unhinderedly" or "without any hindrance." There is a note of victory as he pictures Paul, the missionary to the Gentiles, welcoming all who come to him, "proclaiming the Kingdom of God, and teaching the things concerning the Lord Jesus Christ with all boldness, unhinderedly"[7] (Acts 28:31, author's translation).

Luke, the physician, was a scientific man. As a historian and world traveler, he recorded the facts accurately and with restraint, as if he knew that his story might have to "stand up in court" someday. But as a Gentile believer and companion of a great world-minded missionary, he saw beyond the recorded facts. We can almost hear him say to himself as he lays down his pen: "There, I have told the story thus far. But it is only the beginning. God is working out his purpose for all the nations. It began in Jerusalem, and has now reached Rome on its way out to the ends of the earth. The story will not end until the Son of man, judge of the living and the dead, is exalted as Lord of all nations; and the New Israel, the people of God taken from among all the peoples of the earth, shall serve and glorify him forever and ever. Amen!"

Notes

[1] See article by T. C. Smith, *The Broadman Bible Commentary,* Volume 10 (Nashville: Broadman Press, 1970), pp. 6 f.

[2] The statement in Matthew 19:12, "There are also eunuchs who made themselves eunuchs for the sake of the kingdom of heaven," probably applies to persons who voluntarily choose to live a life of celibacy, rather than those who might mutilate their bodies. But the implication is the same. They are eligible for the kingdom.

[3] A free translation of Acts 8:37, margin. The oldest manuscripts lack this verse, but it is probably authentic.

[4] Frank Stagg, *The Book of Acts* (Nashville: Broadman Press, 1955), p. 172.

[5] The term "self-exclusion" has been popularized by Frank Stagg in his excellent commentary on Acts, cited above. See especially pp. 13-17, 227-33, 263-65 for his analysis of "self-exclusion."

[6] Cf. Stagg, *op. cit.,* pp. 198 f.

[7] See Stagg, *op. cit.,* p. 266.

VIII.
Paul and the Plan
of the Ages

"All nations in the purpose of God" was the magnificent obsession of the apostle Paul. No other biblical writer expressed the theme quite so completely. It was the passion of his life.

Paul gloried in his calling as "an apostle to the Gentiles." The literal meaning of the Greek term is "missionary to the nations." So insistent was he on his special call as a missionary to the Gentile nations and so successful were his efforts to take Christ to the Gentiles that he has at times been pictured as the originator of the idea. The claim has been made that Paul "universalized the gospel," applying it to all mankind in a way which its founder, Jesus of Nazareth, never actually intended.

Our purpose in this chapter is therefore twofold: We shall take note of the remarkable contributions Paul made to the spread of the gospel and the interpretation and application of God's universal purpose. At the same time, we must make it perfectly plain that these sweeping ideas and glorious concepts did not originate in the inspired imagination of the apostle, but were based solidly upon Old Testament Scriptures and were traceable directly to Jesus of Nazareth, not only in his mystical appearances to Paul, but also in his earthly ministry and teachings.

Paul was certain that his call as a missionary (apostle)

came as a sovereign act of God. Six of his letters begin with the salutation, "Paul, an apostle by the will of God."[1] In his letter to the Galatians he expressed the conviction that God had set him apart from his mother's womb, with a foreordained purpose that he should preach Christ among the Gentiles (Gal. 1:15-16). Again and again he referred to the truth of the Gospel as a *stewardship* entrusted to him in the expectation that he would pass it on to the Gentiles.[2]

Much has been made of Paul's statement in Galatians 1:12 that he did not receive the gospel from men but "through a revelation of Jesus Christ."

This does not mean that Paul was preaching a different gospel from that which was being preached by Peter and the other apostles. Paul insisted that he had a calling from God which was not dependent upon a commission from the apostles and elders in Jerusalem. To emphasize this, he declared that he did not even consult with them immediately after his conversion, but went away to Arabia for three years of solitude and preparation. He does admit, however, that he spent fifteen days with Simon Peter afterward, and there can be little doubt that during those days he absorbed all that Peter could tell him of the life and teachings of Jesus (Gal. 1:18). Furthermore, at the time of the Jerusalem conference, Paul submitted to the leaders of the Jerusalem church "the gospel which I preach among the Gentiles" (Gal. 2:2) and no serious questions were raised. On the contrary, as Paul records, it was recognized that he had been entrusted with the gospel for the Gentiles, just as Peter was for the Jews. It was the same gospel, and they shook hands on the understanding that Paul and Barnabas would take it to the Gentiles while Peter and other apostles concentrated their efforts at that time among the Jews (Gal. 2:7-9).

In his first letter to the Corinthian church, Paul, away from the heat of the controversy over his apostleship, freely admitted that he had received from others the heart of the gospel which he preached to them: namely, "that Christ died for our sins according to the Scriptures, and that He was buried, and that He was raised on the third day according to the Scriptures, and that He appeared to Cephas [Peter], then to the twelve. After that He appeared to more than five hundred brethren at one time, most of whom remain until now, but some have fallen asleep; then He appeared to James, then to all the apostles; and last of all, as it were to one untimely born, He appeared to me also" (1 Cor. 15:3-8).

Only the last point would depend upon Paul's Damascus road encounter and his later mystical experiences. The core of his message was the testimony of eyewitnesses of the crucifixion and resurrection, both of which Paul contended were according to the Scriptures. His summary of the Gospel to the Corinthians corresponds closely to Luke's statement of the summary Jesus himself gave to his disciples on the evening of the resurrection day (Luke 24:44-49), and it should be remembered that Luke was a constant companion of Paul during much of the time following his Macedonian call at Troas (Acts 16:9-10). All the facts recorded in Luke's Gospel were readily available to Paul, even if they were not put in final written form until after the death of the apostle.

Paul's dependence upon the Old Testament was recorded again and again in the book of Acts. At Thessalonica he reasoned with the people from the Scriptures, "explaining and giving evidence that the Christ [the Messiah] had to suffer and rise from the dead" (Acts

17:2-3). At Berea he led them to examine the Scriptures daily to see whether his teachings were true (Acts 17:10-11). In his defense before Agrippa, Paul declared, "I stand to this day testifying both to small and great, stating nothing but what the Prophets and Moses said was going to take place; that the Christ was to suffer, and that by reason of His resurrection from the dead He should be the first to proclaim light both to the Jewish people and to the Gentiles" (Acts 26:22-23).

It is clear that Paul did not claim to have discovered some startling new truth: that God's grace and forgiveness was available to Gentiles as well as to Jews. He found it in the Scriptures, and declared that Jesus, the Messiah, had revealed and expounded it for the first time. He did not place himself above his Master, and would have been the first to disclaim that his application of the gospel was wider than Jesus himself had specifically taught.

Paul's Missionary Letters

Thirteen of Paul's letters have been preserved in the New Testament. Each one is directly related to his missionary labors. Several are addressed to churches he had founded, which had to grapple with the question of the relationship of Jewish believers and Gentile converts within their membership. It is not possible to review the teachings of each letter separately. Rather we shall note several recurrent themes which run like golden threads throughout the writings of Paul: (1) that the fullness of salvation was revealed to the Jews first; (2) that it was from the beginning intended for the Gentiles also; (3) that the all-inclusiveness of God's love and forgiveness was first clearly revealed by the Messiah himself; and (4) that this was all according to a divine plan conceived before the foundation of the earth and destined to be accomplished as the climax of history.

To the Jew First

Despite the breadth of his sympathies and the completeness of his dedication to the universality of the gospel, Paul never ceased to marvel that in his sovereign wisdom God had seen fit to choose the Jews as instruments for achieving his purpose for all mankind. He was equally certain that God would somehow preserve a spiritual priority for them as "first among equals." Paul had never heard the modern jingle:

> How odd of God
> To choose the Jews!

But he recognized the profound truth it expresses, both as a spiritual paradox and as an historical fact.

This is stated most clearly in Romans 2:9-10. It is important to notice that the Jews were first not only in privilege, but also in responsibility; not only for honor, but also for judgment. It is only a matter of priority. In the end there is no real difference, for God will treat all nations alike. But the priority is there:

There will be tribulation and distress for every soul of man who does evil, of the Jew first and also of the Greek. / But glory and honor and peace to every man who does good, to the Jew first and also the Greek.

The priority of the Jews is also recognized in Ephesians 1:12-13. Here it is necessary to notice carefully Paul's use of the personal pronouns, "we" and "you." In verse 12, he identifies himself with his Jewish people, in contrast with "you Gentiles," even though in the verses immediately preceding he had spoken of all Christians, both

Jews and Gentiles, as "we" and "us." His readers, mostly Gentile believers, understood the changing emphases, as Paul used the pronouns first in the general, inclusive sense, and then in the particular, nationalistic sense. A paraphrase of the passage beginning at verse 5 brings out the contrast:

He predestines us (all of us, both Jews and Gentiles) to adoption as sons through Jesus Christ.

In Him we (all of us) have redemption through His blood.

He made known to us (both Jews and Gentiles) the mystery of His will.

Also we (all of us) have obtained an inheritance, according to His purpose.

To the end that we (we Jews), who were the first to hope in Christ (that is, hope for the Messiah) should be to the praise of His glory.

In Him, you also (you Gentiles), after listening to the message of truth, the good news that you too can be saved, have believed and received the Holy Spirit, which God promised as the seal, His stamp of acceptance and ownership, indicating that you, too, belong to Him.

Paul was doubtless familiar with the saying of Jesus, "Many who are first will be last; and the last, first (Matt. 19:30; 20:16), although he never quoted it. As a devout Jew who loved his own people and was burdened for their spiritual welfare, he was deeply concerned lest the Jews be left out altogether, as he saw the Gentiles responding in such large numbers and the Jews hardening their hearts against the gospel. In distress of soul, he raised the question, "Has God rejected his people, the Hebrews?" (Rom. 11:1, author's paraphrase). Quickly he went on to deny that this could be so, pointing out that at least a remnant had believed, as so often in the past. He then expressed the confidence that this hardening was not only partial, but was also temporary, "until the fullness of the Gentiles has come in" (Rom. 11:25), after which "all Israel will be saved," meaning apparently that there will be a massive turning to Christ of those who are Israelites by birth and nationality.[3] Many Christians share this hope and pray for the day when it will happen. But in the meantime, they recognize with Paul that, until God in his own sovereign wisdom sees fit to act, in this present age of witnessing, "there is no distinction between Jew and Greek, for the same Lord is Lord of all abounding in riches for all who call upon him" (Rom. 10:12).

"There Is No Difference"

Paul employs several figures of speech to show how, in spite of the obvious priority of the Jews, there is now no real difference in the spiritual status of the individual Jew and Gentile. We note two of his most telling illustrations: one from the area of family life, and the other from the sociopolitical realm.

(1) The son and the household slaves. In order to assure the Galatian Gentiles that they were not inferior to "the sons of Abraham," as the Judaizers contended, Paul told a parable readily understandable to those who had often seen wealthy homes with one pampered child served by a host of household servants. In his parable, there was an only child, who was supposed to be the sole heir of his father's estate. As a minor, he had not entered into the inheritance, so it was only a future hope. His father had placed the boy under the care of household slaves, who actually had authority over him in many matters. The child had no real advantage over the slaves, who had full use of the household and were well fed and

cared for by their master. Perhaps they stood in awe of the youth, thinking that one day he would inherit the estate and they would then be his slaves. But as it turned out, to the surprise of all, when the owner's will was read, it was discovered that he had legally adopted all his household slaves and named them as joint-heirs, along with the "son," who had expected to become the sole heir. As a further surprise, it was revealed that the supposed heir was not really a son after all, but needed to be adopted so that he might share the inheritance. So there had really been no difference all along, either in the mind of the master, or in the degree of freedom and opportunity that all members of the household enjoyed. The distinctions were temporary and only nominal. As soon as the master's will was made public, all distinctions were wiped out. All the former slaves were made sons, and the one who thought he was a natural son was also adopted. All were coheirs, adopted sons with equal status in the household of the gracious master.

Once again it is important to notice Paul's use of the personal pronouns, referring as he does at times to the Jews, at times to Gentile believers, and again to all believers together. With this background, let us paraphrase Galatians 4:1-7:

Now let me point out that as long as an heir is a minor, he has no real advantage over a slave in the same household, even though he is technically the owner of everything. For he is placed under guardians and house managers, who supervise his activities and limit his freedom up to the time he becomes of age. In similar fashion, we Jews, while we were children (prior to the coming of the Messiah) were under restrictions, subject to the same moral principles which apply to all men (and also being under the Mosaic Law). But when the fullness of time came, God sent forth His Son, born of

woman, born under the Law, in order that He might redeem
those who were under the Law, so that we (Jews) might be
adopted as sons. And as evidence that you Gentiles are sons
also, God sent the Holy Spirit, the Spirit of His Son, into your
hearts, so that you Gentiles and we Jews alike cry out, "Abba!"
"Father!"

So since you Gentiles have had the same experience as we
Jewish believers had, the Spirit gives you the inner witness
that you are children of God. Therefore, each of you Gentiles
is no longer a slave, but a son, and if a son, then an heir
through the gracious act of God, with exactly the same status
as the Jewish believer.

(2) Citizens and aliens. In the Ephesian letter, Paul used
an illustration from the political realm. He compared
Gentile Christians with aliens who had no citizenship
and were regarded as outsiders, whereas the Jews were
thought to be citizens of the commonwealth of God. Indeed, Gentiles had been considered enemies, at war with
God's people. But the coming of the Messiah changed
all that. He broke down the barrier between Jew and
Gentile, identifying himself with all mankind, claiming
all without distinction. By his death, he reconciled the
two warring groups, bringing about peace and bestowing
citizenship upon those who had been considered aliens.
To do this, he had to announce peace to the Gentile
nations (as Zech. 9:10 prophesied), but also to proclaim
peace to the Jews, as Isaiah 57:19 predicted.

Again, let us paraphrase and amplify the passage in
Ephesians 2:11-19:

Therefore remember that you Gentile believers were at one
time separate from Christ, excluded from the commonwealth
of Israel and aliens to the covenants of promise, having no
hope and without God in the world.
But now in Christ Jesus you who were formerly far away

outside the heavenly city have been brought up close and then inside the city gates at the price of the blood of Christ.

For He Himself is the one who reconciled us and made of the factions one, breaking down the wall that separated us and dispelling the hostility caused by legalistic commandments and peculiar ordinances, in order that He might create one new kind of humanity,[4] thus establishing peace, and that He might reconcile both groups to God, making of them one new body, by means of the cross, and putting an end to the enmity which had existed between them.

As Isaiah said, "He came and preached peace to you (the Gentiles), who were far away, and to us (the Jews), who were near. For through Him we both now have access to God the Father by the activity of the same Holy Spirit. So you Gentiles are no longer strangers and aliens, but are now fellow-citizens along with all true believers. You are members of the household of God.

So again the inspired apostle declared, "There is no difference between the Jew and the Gentile." Gentile believers are not second-class citizens or aliens, but full citizens of the kingdom of God.

The Mystery of the Messiah

No one was more surprised to discover this than Paul himself. He had been certain that the Hebrews were God's Chosen People, divinely ordained to occupy a distinctive place. As a Pharisee, he had been zealous for the Law, meticulous in observing the rituals, carefully guarding against defilement by contact with unclean, uncircumcised Gentiles. He was enraged by Stephen's speech which threatened a breakdown of the traditional barriers.

Having calmly looked on as Stephen was stoned, he obtained letters of authorization to track down others who were promoting this heresy up in Damascus. It was the Lord himself who stopped Paul in his tracks, saying,

"Stephen was right. In opposing this new teaching, you are fighting against God himself. When I died on the cross, it was not as a defeated Jewish Messiah, whose plans for a military revolt against Rome had been thwarted. I was the Suffering Servant foretold by Isaiah. My Father made it clear that it was too small a thing for me only to restore the Kingdom to Israel. He said, 'I will also make you a light for the Gentiles, so that my salvation may reach to the ends of the earth.' As I told my disciples, God's plan is that repentance for forgiveness of sin should be proclaimed in my name to all the nations, and I have chosen you to be one of my witnesses" (author's paraphrase of Isa. 49:6).

How much was communicated in that first blinding encounter with the glorified Christ we can never know. Perhaps it was only the unassailable fact that Jesus was indeed alive from the dead, and that consequently the testimony of his disciples concerning all that he had said and done during his earthly ministry must be accepted. Undoubtedly Paul later searched the Scriptures for himself, with new insight into these messianic passages which Jesus had interpreted to his followers. Added to this was that fifteen-day conference with Simon Peter, and then additional visions and revelations of the Lord which were granted him (2 Cor. 12:1-4). He knew that his Lord was that same Jesus, who had denounced the Pharisees, cleansed the court of the Gentiles, called himself "the Son of man," and fulfilled all that was written in the Scriptures about the Messiah.

At the heart of what was communicated to Paul was what he called "the mystery of the Messiah." The Greek word, *musterion,* commonly used in the so-called "mystery religions," denotes a profound spiritual truth known only to the initiated. For Paul it meant a secret truth, long known to God but largely hidden from men, now fully revealed and widely proclaimed as "an open secret." In seven passages in four different letters, the word has this technical meaning (Rom. 16:25; 1 Cor. 2:7; Eph. 1:9; 3:3,9; Col. 1:26; 4:3). In two passages the full expression in the Greek is "the mystery of the Christ," with the article before Christ (Eph. 3:3; Col. 4:3), indicating that the word here is not a personal name, but the title, which is the Greek equivalent of "Messiah." So the best translation would be "the Mystery of the Messiah," by which Paul means the surprising, unexpected truth about the Messiah and his mission—something other than what most men expected and, especially for Paul, something that had previously been hidden, so that he just could not see it.

To the Corinthians Paul wrote, "We speak God's wisdom in a mystery, the hidden wisdom, which God predestined before the ages of our glory; the wisdom which none of the rulers of this age has understood; for if they had understood it, they would not have crucified the Lord of glory" (1 Cor. 2:7-8).

If the chief priests had understood God's purpose for the Messiah, they would not have turned Jesus over to Pilate. If Pilate had understood, he would not have ordered the crucifixion. The mystery has to do with the world mission of the Messiah!

In the closing benediction of this letter to the Romans, Paul prayed:

Now to Him who is able to establish you according to my gospel and the preaching of Jesus Christ, according to the revelation of the mystery which has been kept secret for long ages past, but now is manifested [openly revealed], and by the Scriptures of the prophets, according to the commandment of the eternal God, has been made known to all the nations, leading [them] to obedience of faith, to the only wise God, through Jesus Christ, be the glory forever. Amen (Rom. 16:25-27).

So the mystery, although long kept secret and not generally understood, was right there in the writings of the prophets all the time. Now at last by God's command it is to be proclaimed to all the nations, so that they may be led to obey and to accept by faith the promised Messiah.

To the Colossians, most of whom were Gentile believers, Paul wrote concerning his suffering for their sake, as he carried out the stewardship which had been entrusted to him for their benefit. This meant proclaiming "the mystery which has been hidden from the past ages and generations; but has now been manifested [revealed] to His saints, to whom God willed to make known what is the riches of the glory of this mystery among the Gentiles, which is Christ in you, [you Gentiles as well as you Jewish believers, meaning all nations] the hope of glory" (Col. 1:26-27).

At the close of his Colossian letter, Paul requested prayer, "that God may open up to us a door for the word, so that we may speak forth the mystery of [the Messiah], for which I have been imprisoned" (Col. 4:3). So it was for proclaiming "the mystery of the Messiah" that Paul was persecuted and imprisoned! What then specifically was "the mystery of the Messiah?" For the definite answer we must turn to the Ephesian letter.

Paul mentioned the mystery in the very introduction to Ephesians, apparently assuming that his readers understood the reference. But at chapter 3, as he was about to offer a prayer on behalf of the Gentile believers, he paused, apparently realizing that they may not yet fully comprehend the wonder of what God has done for them. He reminded them that he was in prison because of his ministry among the Gentiles, and asked them bluntly, "Do you really understand that glorious mystery which was made known to me by revelation, about which I have previously written you, so that you should be able to understand? True, it was not made known to mankind in general in previous generations; not as fully as it has now been revealed to the holy apostles and prophets by the Holy Spirit. This is the mystery now fully revealed: that the Gentiles are fellow-heirs of the Kingdom (along with the Jews); and fellow-members of the body of Christ, the Church; and fellow-partakers of the promise of eternal life in Christ Jesus through the Gospel" (Eph. 3:2-6, author's words).

That is the mystery of the Messiah! He was never intended for Jews alone, but for all mankind! It was his secret, not understood even by his own disciples, until after his death and resurrection. But he announced it to them, revealing what had been a hidden truth in Moses, and in the Prophets, and in the Psalms. He then commanded them to proclaim it to all the nations. When the original apostles seemed a bit slow in carrying out his instructions, he commandeered Paul on the Damascus road and enlisted him in the glorious task of letting all men know that they were included in God's plan of redemption, and that Christ had died for them too.

Ephesians 3:6 is a beautiful poetical statement of the privileges guaranteed to the Gentiles, based upon the Greek word *sun,* which means "with," "jointly," or "together." The alliterative words, all compounds beginning with *su-,* are *sugkleronoma, sussoma,* and *summetocha,* meaning literally "together-heirs," "together-body," and "to-gether-sharers" (of the promises). Everything that the Messiah made available for the Jews is jointly shared with all the other nations on an equal basis of together-ness and unity. It could hardly be stated more forcefully. Every Gentile can say with joyful assurance, "Jesus included me!"

Paul wanted his Gentile friends to know that the world mission of the Messiah made them fully eligible for every blessing given to the Jews, on the basis of faith in the Messiah (the Christ). This he did not originate or discover for himself. It was revealed to him, almost against his will, by the Messiah himself, by Christ, both on the road to Damascus and in the Scriptures, which he had purpose-fully fulfilled!

The Plan of the Ages

In this same glorious third chapter of Ephesians Paul developed another idea to its highest point: "the Plan of the Ages." He used the Greek noun, *prothesis,* in several other places (Rom. 8:28; Eph. 1:11; 2 Tim. 1:9), but only in Ephesians 3:11 is it combined with *ton aionon,* "the ages," *"aeons,"* or "eternity." The resulting phrase is usually translated, "the eternal purpose," but was rendered "The Plan of the Ages" by W. O. Carver, who more than any other in his generation popularized Paul's profound concept.[5]

The term conveys the thought that this is what God had in mind from the beginning. It was no afterthought, but a firm purpose, deliberately decided upon by God himself, and kept constantly in the divine mind through the ages. "The Plan of the Ages" is essentially the same as "the mystery of the Messiah," but expresses the viewpoint of God, the Father, rather than of Christ, the Son. It is Paul's deepest insight into the mind of God, an insight stated in John 3:16: "For God so loved the world, that He gave His only begotten Son, that whoever believes in Him should not perish, but have eternal life." It is the insight which led Carver to write: "The origin of missions is *ultimately* to be found in the heart of God."[6]

Three glorious facts about the Plan of the Ages are contained in Ephesians 3:10-11: (1) the plan was built around the Suffering Messiah; (2) it is to be achieved through the church; and (3) it will result in the complete vindication of God's marvelous wisdom.

"In accordance with the Plan of the Ages, which was made (or formed) around the Messiah, Jesus our Lord"— this is a literal translation of Ephesians 3:11. The presence of the article before "Christ" indicates that his messianic office is intended, rather than a personal title. God the Father foresaw the necessity of suffering to make atonement for sin. That is why there could be only one answer to the prayer of Jesus in Gethsemane, "My Father, if it is possible, let this cup pass from me" (Matt. 26:39), and why Jesus repeatedly said it was *necessary* for the Messiah to suffer and die (Luke 18:31; 24:26,28-46). There was no other way, for "God was in Christ reconciling the world to Himself" (2 Cor. 5:19). He planned it so from the beginning.

The church is to be the means of the final achievement of God's eternal purpose: "in order that the manifold wisdom of God might now be made known through the church" (Eph. 3:10). This has a two-fold meaning. As the church is faithful to the Great Commission, witnessing to the people of the earth, it serves as the agency through which the Plan of the Ages will be accomplished.

This ennobles the missionary enterprise, and makes the witnessing of each individual church member significant. God has seen fit to make his people partners in the work of world redemption.

But the church is more than an agent of evangelization. It is the embodiment of God's ideal—the living demonstration of his wisdom and grace. No one who sees the transformed lives, the loving fellowship of those who have been redeemed by the blood of the Lamb can deny the wisdom of God in providing the marvelous saving grace revealed in Jesus Christ on the cross.

To whom is this demonstration of God's wisdom directed? Not only to scoffers and critics in this world, but "to rulers and the authorities in the heavenly places"[7] (Eph. 3:10), to every intelligent being in the universe, many of whom may have been looking on from distant planets, galaxies, or spiritual realms beyond our knowledge, to see what might happen on planet earth. Here God began his great experiment, creating man in his own image, with freedom of will, the power of choice, the possibility of rebelling against his Maker. Through the ages angelic beings, the principalities and powers in heavenly places, may have wondered sadly whether God had made a mistake in allowing the human race to continue, as they viewed the crime, rebellion, injustice, war and violence going on upon the earth. Demonic forces even now seem to be mocking God and challenging his patience and wisdom. But God has a plan. It centers in the Christ of the cross; and one day the church, the beautiful bride of Christ, redeemed, purified, and glorious, will stand as God's complete vindication. Every being in the universe will have to confess that God was right in taking the chance involved in the creation of Man, as free human beings, from every race and nation, re-deemed and transformed, controlled by the Holy Spirit, freely serve him with praise and thanksgiving, in the name of his son, the Savior of the world!

This is the Plan of the Ages. It cannot fail. And we are a part of the plan!

Notes

[1] First and 2 Corinthians, Ephesians, Colossians, 2 Timothy, Titus.

[2] First Corinthians 4:1-2; Ephesians 3:2; Colossians 1:25-27. The word *dispensation* in the King James Version should be "stewardship."

[3] See Romans 11:16. It is not at all certain that the statement, "all Israel will be saved," means that at some point the whole nation of Israel and all who have Jewish blood in their veins will recognize Jesus as the Messiah. In Romans 9:6-8, Paul declared, "For they are not all Israel, who are descended from Israel, neither are they all children because they are Abraham's descendants." He distinguishes between the natural Israel and the spiritual Israel, the true Israel, composed of Jews and Gentiles alike. This may be the meaning of the term in Romans 11:26, although the context suggests that Paul foresees a time when all the natural Israel will become a part of the spiritual Israel. Like Paul, we can only hope and pray that this will happen, and leave it to the mercy and wisdom of God. (See Rom. 11:33-36.)

[4] The Greek word in verse 15 is *anthropos* = "man"; literally, "one new man," meaning one new race or kind of humanity. Thus in a surprise twist to his analogy, Paul made the point that not even the Jews were natural-born citizens of the commonwealth of God, but some taken from among the Jews were made into a new kind of people.

[5] In his book, *Missions in the Plan of the Ages,* and also in *The Glory of God in the Christian Calling,* a commentary on Ephesians.

[6] *Missions in the Plan of the Ages,* p. 12.

[7] Ephesians 3:10, NASB, "the principalities and powers in the heavenly places," KJV and RSV.

IX.
The Missionary Consummation

Our study of the theme, "All Nations in the Purpose of God," has led us through the Old Testament, the Gospels, Acts, and the writings of Paul. This "golden thread" might be traced through the remainder of the Bible, for even in writings addressed primarily to Jewish believers (as are Hebrews, James, and perhaps the epistles of Peter) the setting is universal rather than nationalistic. Christ is recognized as the Lord of glory, who sits at the right hand of the Majesty on high (Heb. 1:3; 9:24), who has an eternal priesthood, far above the Levitical priests, who has formed the new Chosen People (1 Pet. 2:9-10), and established an eternal kingdom open to all by faith (2 Pet. 1:1-11).

First John 2:2 makes the universal purpose quite specific: "He Himself is the propitiation for our sins; and not for ours only, but also for those of *the whole world*" (author's italics). Third John, although quite brief, is a classic argument for the material support of missionaries, who go out "taking nothing from the Gentiles" whom they are seeking to win, and who deserve to be supported by the church "in a manner worthy of God," in order that those who support them "may be fellow-workers in the truth" (3 John 5-8).

The universal sweep of the Revelation is inescapable,

and to that we shall come shortly. But first let us raise the question, How will it all end? Does the Bible give any clear answer to the riddle of history, and definite assurance that Christians are on the winning side in the cosmic struggle for the souls of men?

The Eschatology of Jesus

To begin with, let us examine what Jesus himself said about the nature and the growth of the Kingdom, about the judgment of Israel and the other nations, and about his return and the end of the age.

It is clear from the Scriptures that the kingdom of God is not material, territorial, or political. Jesus said, "My kingdom is not of this world" (John 18:36). He also said, "The kingdom of God is not coming with signs to be observed" (Luke 17:20), but is within you, or right in your midst (Luke 17:21).[1] He spoke of persons entering the kingdom after meeting certain spiritual conditions (Matt. 19:24), and to a certain lawyer he said, "You are not far from the kingdom" (Mark 12:34), obviously referring to a spiritual condition, rather than to spatial proximity. The primary meaning of the term, "Kingdom of God," is a spiritual realm to be entered by faith by persons living here on earth. This is the Kingdom which true believers receive as an inheritance (1 Cor. 6:9; 15:50; Gal. 5:21; Eph. 5:5). It was inaugurated by the death of Jesus Christ, and is the free gift of God. As Jesus assured his anxious disciples, "Do not be afraid, little flock, for your Father has chosen gladly to give you the kingdom" (Luke 12:32).

At the same time, in almost paradoxical fashion, Jesus spoke of the growth of the Kingdom and was concerned for its extension throughout the world, both in terms

of space and of time. In a series of parables, he taught
that the Kingdom is like mustard seed, very small at
first, but destined to grow until it is quite large (Matt.
13:31-32). Like leaven, it will spread silently, but surely,
by a process of permeation (Matt. 13:33). Again and again
there is the inference that the process of growth will
move to a grand climax, a dramatic finale on a worldwide
stage.

One of the most remarkable parables of the Kingdom
is the story of the tares sown among the wheat by an
enemy of the owner. In explaining the parable to his
disciples later, Jesus declared:

The one who sows the good seed is the Son of Man, and
the field is the world; and as for the good seed, these are the
sons of the kingdom; and the tares are the sons of the evil
one; and the enemy who sowed them is the devil, and the
harvest is the end of the age; and the reapers are angels (Matt.
13:37-39).

This clearly pictures Christ on a cosmic scale, scattering
his own people throughout the world, to live and work
side by side with the sons of the devil until the time
of judgment at the end of the age. Then the separation
takes place. Before that time it is not always possible
to tell the difference between the wheat and the tares
(sons of the Kingdom and sons of the devil). So, as in
the parable, the owner tells his servants not to try to
pull up the tares, lest they uproot some of the wheat,
Jesus taught his disciples that the good and the bad will
be allowed to grow together until God's time of judgment.
Christians are not to judge, but to leave the judgment
to God, who will make no mistakes in his righteous judgment. There is no promise that all persons in the world
will ever in this age be won to faith in Christ. But it

was the clear intention of Jesus that his representatives be distributed throughout the world in this age as witnesses. It was Jesus who said, "The field is the world," just as he said, "The harvest is the end of the age" (Matt. 13:38-39).

That the final judgment is to be worldwide, including all the nations, is made clear in another beautiful but terrifying statement of our Lord:

But when the Son of Man comes in His glory, and all the angels with Him, then will He sit on His glorious throne.

And all the nations will be gathered before Him; and He will separate them from one another, as the shepherd separates the sheep from the goats; and He will put the sheep on His right, and the goats on the left (Matt. 25:31-33).

This prophecy has been quoted many times to emphasize the words that follow: "Inasmuch as ye have done it unto one of the least of these my brethren, ye have done it unto me" (Matt. 25:40, KJV). The implication is that the way to please God is to feed the hungry, clothe the naked, visit the sick and those in prison. Those who use this passage to magnify the place of social service often gloss over the teaching that the service to be rewarded is not on behalf of mankind in general, but "to one of these brothers of Mine, even the least of them" (Matt. 25:40); that is, to one of the true followers of Jesus. He here identifies himself with the little band of disciples, and with others who become members of his body, the continuing incarnation on earth. The standard of judgment becomes not mere humanitarian service, but the attitude toward Christ, the recognition of him and his people. The Kingdom to be received by the righteous was prepared for them "from the foundation of the world," and is to be received as an inheritance, not earned by good works. The recipients are to be identified by their actions, which are the result of their nature; performed not for reward but in self-giving sacrificial service, because of the kind of persons they have become as a result of God's redeeming grace. Furthermore, while the judgment is to be on an individual basis, it is dramatically set in the context of a universal event, when *all the nations* will be gathered before Christ, as the judge of the nations.

Matthew 24

From the very beginning of his ministry, Jesus had been calling for national repentance, warning that the nation of Israel was under judgment and would soon be destroyed if there was not a widespread change of heart. During the last week in Jerusalem, he saw that it was too late. He wept over the city and quietly predicted to his disciples that the Temple buildings would be completely destroyed. That evening his disciples came to him privately and begged, "Tell us, when will these things be, and what will be the sign of Your coming, and of the end of the age?" (Matt. 24:3). The remainder of the twenty-fourth chapter of Matthew is the most complete statement Jesus made about future events.[2] This passage is not easily understood, and has been the source of many different interpretations. While no detailed exposition is possible here, several salient facts should be noted.

The question asked by the disciples has three parts. In his account of Jesus' reply, Matthew does not always make clear which of the three questions was being answered. He seems to alternate between the timing of the destruction of Jerusalem and the end of the age. As a result, many have tried to make the words of Jesus apply to a single great event. Careful analysis of his words reveals that he must have been speaking of at least two different events, and possibly three: the destruction of the Temple, his own return, and the end of the age.

In answer to the question, "When will the Temple be destroyed?" Jesus replied, "It will be soon. Before this generation passes away it will happen. Some of you may be in Jerusalem at that time. If so, flee from the city, for God will not spare it. Indeed, if you are anywhere in Judea, flee to the hills; for it will be an awful time of destruction, and I am warning you in advance."

To the question, "What will be the sign of your coming and of the end of the age," the answer seems to have been: "That will not be as soon as you might think. Do not be misled. After my death, many will come saying, 'I am the Messiah.' But these will be false pretenders. Don't let them fool you. There will be wars, famines, and earthquakes. But do not think that every great upheaval is the sign of the end. No, there must be time for the good news of the Kingdom to be preached throughout the world, among all the nations. After that the end will come. As for my return, there will be no doubt about it when it occurs. It will not be something secret or concealed, but like a flash of lightning, which illuminates the entire world from east to west. All the nations will be aware of it, and those who are not prepared for my coming will mourn, while my own people will rejoice.

"I cannot tell you when this will happen," he plainly stated. "I do not know. Not even the angels in heaven know the exact time. Only My heavenly Father knows. There is only one thing for you to do: Be alert. Be ready.

Be busy doing what I have told you to do. Always be
ready, for it could happen at any time (author's paraphrase of Matt. 24:4-44).

The prediction of the fall of Jerusalem and the destruction of the Temple was fulfilled with terrible exactness
in the year A.D. 70. Nationalist zealots had rebelled in
A.D. 66, and the patience of the Roman leaders was ex-
hausted. Reinforcements were sent to strengthen the
army of occupation, and as the Jewish extremists resisted
with fanatical determination, the Roman generals decided
to put down the rebellion once for all. Judea was completely overrun, until only the walled city of Jerusalem
remained. A long, bitter siege began in A.D. 68, just after
the few Christians who remained fled across the Jordan
to Pella and thus survived the holocaust. The Jewish gar-
risons held out stubbornly until at last, weakened by
starvation and disease, they were overwhelmed by the
Roman forces. Huge battering rams penetrated the walls
at points, and a murderous horde poured in and slaughtered the surviving defenders in a bloody orgy.

In one sense the fall of Jerusalem and the destruction
of the Temple constituted a "coming of the Son of man"
in judgment upon the nation which had rejected him
and brought about his crucifixion. It did mark "the end
of the age" for the nation of Israel, which was not to
be restored to anything resembling freedom and independence until the end of the Palestinian crisis in 1948.
It could be that in those last tragic hours of Jerusalem's
agony, some of the defenders may have looked up to
heaven and caught a vision of Jesus at the right hand
of God, even as Stephen had seen him while he was
being stoned! But we have no record of this, and it seems
more likely that the predictions of his coming looked

down the centuries, beyond the judgment of Israel to the final judgment of all the nations, an event which is still in the future.

This being the case, the admonitions of our Lord to his disciples have been equally applicable to every generation of believers, and still constitute a warning and a challenge to Christians today: "Be ready. Be busy. Obey your instructions, for the end could come at any time." And what has he told us to do, in order to be ready for his return and our time of judgment?

As we have seen, the risen Lord made it perfectly plain in repeated appearances over the space of forty days before his ascension: "You are not to be concerned about times and seasons which the Heavenly Father has reserved within his own sovereign authority. But you are to be witnesses for me wherever you are, both at home and abroad, extending into all the world, among all the nations. You are to witness faithfully, both by word and deed, letting me live on in you through the living presence of the Holy Spirit. He will tell you what to do and what to say. Bear witness to me, and leave the results to God. Some will hear and respond gladly; others will resist and reject your message, just as they did when I was in their midst in fleshly form.

"In this present age not all will be won, but it is my Father's good pleasure to take some from among every race, tribe, language, and culture, and to blend them into one new kind of humanity, the New Israel, the New People of God. By the grace of God, you have been chosen to be a member of this people, and have been entrusted with the good news intended to reach others who have not yet learned of my Father's love and forgiveness. Your time of opportunity may be short. I may come in final judgment soon. Be faithful to the end, and I will grant you entrance into the eternal Kingdom, which my Father has prepared for you."[3]

The Revelation of John

The last book of the Bible is an appropriate climax and conclusion to the amazing record of God's loving purpose for all the nations of the earth. To some it has been a book of riddles and a source of confusion. When properly understood, it becomes a source of joy, an assurance of victory, and a challenge to faithful witnessing.

The Revelation of John was probably written about A.D. 95 in the midst of severe persecution against the churches of the Roman province of Asia. The emperor, Domitian, had proclaimed himself divine, and ordered all his subjects to revere him as "Lord," to prove their loyalty to the empire. This could have been considered a mere patriotic gesture, similar to saluting the flag, and some were tempted to conform. But to the earnest Christians of Asia, it was regarded as a test of faith. They had no Lord but Jesus Christ, and to repeat the simple affirmation, "Caesar is Lord," was blasphemy and heresy. The aged John, exiled on the island of Patmos, wrote to encourage the churches to stand firm and refuse to deny their Lord.

John called his writing an "apocalypse" of Jesus Christ. Often translated "revelation," the Greek word *apokalupsis* literally means "uncovering," "laying bare." It often is associated with the revelation of truth by means of ecstatic visions. Apocalyptic literature makes use of symbols, numerology, and cryptic language designed to be understood only by those with spiritual insight. John used this method of communication partly to avoid creating further difficulties for his readers, even then under the threat of persecution. The assurance that their enemies were doomed to defeat was stated in veiled language.

It is generally agreed that the various beasts and evil personalities described in the Revelation would be readily recognized by first-century Christians as persons then living or soon to appear. They would understand that John was predicting the fall of the Roman Empire, and of course this did eventually occur. John's immediate purpose was to comfort and sustain believers in that generation with the assurance that God was on their side, and the ultimate outcome was not in doubt. In so doing, he shared insights and expressed universal spiritual truths which far transcended his own time, and have brought strength and hope to many generations of Christians, especially during times of trouble.

The modern reader of the Revelation will do well to avoid trying to identify the various animals and symbols or to chart the future according to time schedules suggested. Rather, the spiritual message of the book as a whole should be sought, and the universal redemptive purpose of God underscored.

In a series of visions in groups of seven the trials and tribulations undergone by Christians are presented in dramatic fashion. At the climax of each great struggle the living Christ emerges as the victor. The last scene represents the final victory at the end of the age and the eternal destiny of the faithful.

The sweeping scope of the Revelation is breathtaking. It covers the whole world and the entire range of history. Through windows opened to the future, we are allowed to preview coming events: not in minute detail, but in terms of the certain outcome. As one who has read the last chapter of a mystery novel and knows how it will end even while reading each absorbing chapter, so we are given the privilege of glimpsing the end from the beginning.

No detailed analysis of the book is possible here. We can only note some passages in which God's redemptive plan for all the nations is clearly revealed and the ultimate victory of the Righteous One is forecast. We then rejoice in the evangelistic invitation with which the inspired writer closes his message.

Revelation 5:9-10 is the song of the twenty-four elders and the four living creatures addressed to the Lamb of God just before the opening of the scroll with seven seals, representing God's secret plan of redemption, which was not understood until opened and laid bare by the suffering Messiah. The song of praise to the One who made it possible for men to understand the meaning of history makes clear that it all revolves around the eternal purpose of God for all the nations of the earth:

> And they sang a new song, saying,
> "Worthy art Thou to take the book, and to break its seals; for Thou wast slain, and didst purchase for God with Thy blood men from every tribe and tongue and people and nation.
> "And Thou hast made them to be a kingdom and priests to our God; and they will reign upon the earth."

Revelation 7:9-10 is John's vision of the multitude of the redeemed revealed just before the breaking of the seventh seal, completing the unveiling of the mystery of the Messiah. In addition to the 144,000, symbolically representing the limited number of Jews who had believed (12,000 from each of the twelve tribes of Israel), there was a vast multitude, too many even to be counted.

This represents Gentile converts, already numerous in John's day and one day to be countless in number. And note well: they will be from every nation, from all tribes and peoples. Together they stand around the throne of God, all clothed in white robes, with palm branches in their hands, singing praises to God and to the Lamb.

Look more closely at the multitude. The white robes, symbolizing purity and perfection resulting from washing them in the blood of the Lamb, create a sameness in the outward appearance of the worshipers. But if one looks carefully at the faces, there is vast variety. No Japanese kimonos are visible, but one can distinguish bright eyes with an Oriental slant. Indian saris are replaced with white robes, but those slender brown faces must be from Calcutta or Bombay! Colorful African garments are not to be seen, but dark-skinned faces are accented by gleaming white teeth as joyous songs are lifted. It is a multiracial, cosmopolitan assemblage, blended into one huge choir, harmonizing the many languages of the world into one swelling paeon of praise!

Scene after scene appears in the Apocalypse, but none can eclipse this vision of the vast company of the redeemed, except for the spotlighted appearances of Christ himself, who comes in various guises, always the commanding central figure, in complete control of the situation. When the seventh angel sounds his trumpet, loud voices from heaven announce: "The kingdom of the world has become the kingdom of our Lord, and of His Christ; and He will reign forever and ever" (Rev. 11:15).[4] What had been promised in Psalm 2 has now been accomplished, and the Lamb soon stands in triumph on Mount Zion, ruling over the nations (Rev. 14:1; 15:4).

Among the angels flying in the mid-heavens is one

"having an eternal gospel to preach to those who live on the earth, and to every nation and tribe and tongue and people" (Rev. 14:6). His message is a warning that the hour of judgment is at hand, and soon the image of the Lamb is mystically transformed into the form of one like a Son of man, sitting on a cloud, with a golden crown on his head and a sharp sickle in his hand. What was foretold in Daniel 7:13 f. is here fulfilled, and as the angel gives the command, "Put in your sickle and reap, because the hour to reap has come, because the harvest of the earth is ripe" (Rev. 14:15), the parable of the wheat and tares in Matthew 13:37-39 comes to its consummation. The Son of man presides over the final judgment of the nations.

The last appearance of Christ is as a conquering warrior, astride a white horse, clothed with a robe dipped in blood, leading the armies of heaven in triumph. "And from His mouth comes a sharp sword, so that with it He may smite the nations; and He will rule them with a rod of iron. . . . And on His robe and on His thigh He has a name written, 'KING OF KINGS, AND LORD OF LORDS' " (Rev. 19:15-16).

One final effort at rebellion soon ends in failure. Satan is bound and thrown into the lake of fire. Death and all evil are vanquished and a new heaven and new earth come into being. Speculation concerning the thousand year period mentioned in Revelation 20 has proved fruitless. The many theories about the timing of events, based upon a literalistic interpretation of this chapter have been divisive and unproductive.[5] It is best to admit our inability to predict details, and focus upon the central truth: the final victory of the Lord of Righteousness is certain. A new world awaits the faithful. And in the New Jerusalem which will be our dwelling-place, there will be no temple:

> For the Lord God, the Almighty, and the Lamb, are its temple.
> And the city has no need of the sun or of the moon to shine upon it, for the glory of God has illumined it, and its lamp is the Lamb.
> And the nations shall walk by its light, and the kings of earth shall bring their glory into it (Rev. 21:22-23).

All nations in the accomplished purpose of God!

The Revelation closes with a fervent evangelistic invitation, unlimited in its scope:

> The Spirit and the bride say, "Come!"
> And let him who hears say, "Come!"
> Whoever is thirsty, let him come;
> and whoever wishes, let him take the free gift
> of the water of life (Rev. 22:17, NIV).

The Holy Spirit says, "Come!" Surely this is that urgent inner voice seeking to bring conviction and surrender in the heart of every lost person!

The Bride says, "Come!" This is the church, the responsible agency for evangelism and missions, which is constantly inviting others to come and share the joy of salvation.

Let him who hears say, "Come!" Regrettably, not every one who has heard the gospel turns and invites others to go with him in repentance and faith, as he runs to embrace the Savior. But every one should, and here the inspired author of the Revelation urges each one who has heard the good news to pass on the invitation to others.

And who may come? Anyone and everyone! Whoever is thirsty, and feels the need deep within. Whoever wishes and makes up his mind to do so. Whosoever will may come! Regardless of race, culture, language, sex, or spiritual condition, the way is open. The invitation is for ALL!

So, Come! Come quickly, before Christ comes again! For he is coming soon, and his coming will be in judgment upon all who have not believed his word, and made peace with the Prince of Peace, who is also the King of kings, and Lord of lords!

Thus it is written in the Book of Books. And thus ends the glorious story of the Plan of the Ages, the eternal purpose of God for all the nations of the world.

Notes

[1] See marginal reading in NASB.

[2] Mark 13 and Luke 21 are briefer accounts of the same discourse.

[3] The author's free paraphrase of various sayings on the Gospels and Acts.

[4] Revelation 11:15. The King James Version reads "kingdoms," but the Greek word is singular. *Today's English Version* expresses it well: "The power to rule over the world belongs now to our Lord and his Messiah."

[5] For a discussion of the various theories of the millennium, see Herschel Hobbs, *The Cosmic Drama, An Exposition of the Book of Revelation* (Waco: Word Publishers, 1971), pp 13-15, 181-93.

X.
The Unfinished Task

One hundred forty-nine nations are listed as members of the United Nations organization in 1978, ranging in size from the tiny republic of Malta, with about 28,000 citizens, to the Peoples Republic of China, with an estimated population of nearly 800 million. A few small nations are not yet members of the UN, such as Monaco and Liechtenstein. The only sizable countries still outside the world organization are Rhodesia and South-West Africa, both of which may soon be admitted as independent states. The total number of units which might be recognized as "nations" in the full sense of political independence is therefore about 160. This should be kept in mind when one recalls the command of our Lord to go and make disciples of "all the nations."

To disciple 160 nations is a staggering assignment, but the Christian responsibility does not end there, for within those nations are many tribes and "families." The divine commission to Abraham was, "through you and your (spiritual) descendants all the families of the earth shall be blessed" (author's translations of Gen. 12:3; 28:14). And in the great multitude to be gathered around the throne of the Lamb are to be those "from every nation and all tribes and peoples and tongues" (Rev. 7:9). None is to be left out or overlooked!

No one knows exactly how many tribes and languages there are in the world.[1] The usually accepted estimate is about 3,000. At least one book of the Bible has now been translated into over 1,600 different languages and dialects, but it is recognized that more than a thousand tongues remain to be reduced to writing in order that the Bible may be put into those languages.[2]

In Africa alone, 860 tribes have been identified, and because some tribes are divided by the political boundaries of modern nations, a total of 1,045 "tribes-within-nations" are listed by David B. Barrett in his comprehensive survey completed in 1972.[3] Of these, 512 have been evangelized to some extent, while 270 are dominantly Muslim, and 263 others are classified as "unevangelized and resistant."[4]

No comparable study has been made of the unreached tribes of Asia and Latin America, and generalizations are risky, but it can safely be said that not more than half of the tribal and linguistic groups of the earth have been even partially evangelized. Many of the unevangelized tribes are small groups in remote places, but the concern of our Lord for "the least, the last, and the lost" will not permit his followers to ignore those who know nothing of the saving acts of God.

In addition to reaching the entirely unevangelized tribes is the equally challenging task of helping to strengthen the Christians within many of the larger tribes and nations, where churches have been planted, but the believers still constitute a tiny fraction of the population, and need assistance, especially in training and equipping their own leaders for the continuing work of evangelization and Christian nurture.

Before seeking to analyze the world mission situation

for this generation, let us take a quick review of the past, to see how we reached our present status. For the evangelization of even half the peoples of the world was no easy task, and history can teach us some lessons.

The Spread of Christianity Up to 1792

At the close of the New Testament era, Christianity seems almost to have gone underground, as severe persecutions left scant written records of its spread. But despite the fire and sword, gladiatorial combats and life in the catacombs, the vibrant new faith not only survived, but continued to spread, until the conversion of Constantine in A.D. 313 brought a troubled peace. This was a mixed blessing, since it brought also the union of church and state and a consequent loss of spiritual vitality. By the year A.D. 500 Christianity was established as the official religion of the Roman Empire, but its trials had only begun.

Latourette has termed the period from A.D. 500 to 1500 "The Thousand Years of Uncertainty," because its growth was checked and its very survival threatened.[5] Europe was invaded by hordes of pagan tribes, so that territory once "Christianized" had to be reevangelized in a massive series of home mission undertakings. Islam arose in Arabia in A.D. 622, and soon spread across North Africa and into Spain, from whence the Moors were not finally expelled until 1492. The Muslims overran Asia Minor and threatened Constantinople, which at last fell in 1453, exposing eastern Europe to religious wars in reprisal for the Crusades, which had failed to reconquer lost territory in the Holy Land.

Christianity was largely confined to Europe and prevented from reaching the rest of the world by Muslim encirclement, until Columbus found a way to the New World of the Americas in 1492, and six years later Portuguese sailors under Vasco da Gama succeeded where Columbus had failed, sailing around Africa to reach India and China, which had been the ultimate goal of Columbus and the Spanish explorers. A papal decree promptly divided the world between the two Catholic maritime powers, and Spain was charged with responsibility for planting the Catholic church in the Americas, and Portugal in Africa, Asia, and the eastern edge of South America, which became Brazil. For two hundred years, the ships which brought gold from South America and silks and spices from the Orient carried missionary priests and Catholic colonizers to what became Latin America, and to the Orient. After the defeat of the Spanish Armada in 1588, Spain and Portugal were challenged by the Protestant nations, England and Holland, but they lagged far behind in spreading their form of the Faith.

By 1790 Roman Catholicism was well planted in South America, the Caribbean, the Philippines, and Quebec, while Protestant outreach was confined largely to the newly-independent British colonies in North America and Dutch holdings in the East Indies and at the tip of South Africa. There was little consciousness of world responsibility among the Protestant and Evangelical churches of Europe and North America, until the missionary awakening which began in 1792, largely as the result of the vision and determination of William Carey, pastor of the Baptist church at Leicester, England.

Carey did two things to arouse reluctant Christians to action. First, he brought the unevangelized masses of the world to the attention of evangelicals by carefully compiled statistics; and second, he laid the missionary commission of our Lord on the consciences of committed Christians.

No one had bothered to compile accurate, comprehensive religious statistics of the world until an eighty-seven-page booklet by William Carey came from the press in the spring of 1792, under the title: *An Enquiry into the Obligation of Christians to Use Means for the Conversion of the Heathens.* The significant subtitle read: "In which the religious state of the different nations of the world, the success of former undertaking, and the practicability of further undertakings, are considered."

Carey carefully listed by continents every known nation, and such little-known islands as Arroe, Alsen, Mona, Paros, Banda, Buro, and Gillola. For each territory, he gave the length and breadth in miles, the number of inhabitants, and the religious complexion as a whole. Again and again he had to record: "Pagans, Ditto, Mahometans, Pagans, Ditto, Ditto." In summary he found the world population to be 731,000,000, of whom, as he said sadly, "four hundred and twenty millions . . . are still in pagan darkness; an hundred and thirty millions the followers of Mahomet; an hundred millions catholics; forty-four millions protestants; thirty millions of the greek and armenian churches, and perhaps seven millions of jews."[6]

If Carey's figures are correct (and they have never been challenged), the total number of nominal Christians in 1792, including all Catholic, Eastern Orthodox, Protestant, and Evangelical denominations, was about 174,-000,000, or 23.8 percent of the world population. Protestants and Evangelicals constituted some 6 percent of the people of the world, with Carey's own group, the Particular Baptists, numbering not more than 30,000 in some four hundred small churches of England. To these his challenge was specifically directed. As a member of a minority "sect" within a society dominated by a state church, he readily acknowledged pressing needs at home. But his most urgent call was that something be done, "more than what is done, for the conversion of the Heathen."[7]

Carey based his challenge firmly on the Scriptures. His very first chapter was, "An Enquiry whether the Commission given by our Lord to his Disciples be not still binding on us."[8] The heart of his argument was centered on the Great Commission as recorded in Matthew 28:19-20, and was directed against the view then commonly held by Particular Baptists, that the missionary commission was given only to the apostles and did not apply to other disciples then or in succeeding generations. This he refuted by pointing out that, "if the command to teach all nations be restricted to the apostles . . . then that of baptizing should be so too; and every denomination of Christians, except the Quakers, do wrong in baptizing with water at all."[9] His fellow-Baptists had no answer to his question concerning their authority to baptize!

After pointing out that, if his opponents' view were correct, then all efforts to spread the gospel since the time of the apostles was without any divine authority, Carey clinched his argument with this telling statement: "If the command of Christ to teach all nations extend only to the apostles, then, doubtless, the promise of the divine presence in this work must be so limited; but this is worded in such a manner as expressly precludes such an idea. *Lo, I am with you always, to the end of the world.*"[10] In other words, Carey reasoned, just as the promise of Christ's presence applies to all true disciples until the end of the age, so also his command to go and teach all nations must apply to all, and is still binding on Christians today.

Carey's opportunity to call for action came as he preached the official sermon at the annual meeting of the Nottingham Baptist Association on May 30, 1792. Using Isaiah 54:2-3 as a text, he challenged the little churches to lengthen their cords and strengthen their stakes, getting ready to "inherit the Gentiles," as God had promised. "Expect great things from God" and "Attempt great things for God" were his two main points. As a result of the sermon and of his personal insistence following it, plans were made for the matter to be discussed in detail at the next meeting of the ministers of the association. This led to the formation of the Particular Baptist Society for the Propagation of the Gospel Amongst the Heathen on October 2, 1792, the first voluntary organization for foreign missions in modern times.

It was an idea whose hour had come! Despite formidable obstacles, the little society moved forward promptly, and within less than a year, two missionary families were on their way to India, including Carey, his reluctant wife, her sister, and three children. The feeble Baptists had shown that it could be done, and in rapid succession every other denomination followed their pattern of organization and action. The "Modern Missionary Movement" had been launched! The time was ripe, and many factors combined to produce the new awakening. But the catalyst God used was one man who was burdened for the lost multitudes of the world and who believed that the missionary command of our Lord was binding upon him and his fellow Christians!

Progress from 1792 to 1938

The century and a half following the publication of Carey's *Enquiry* and his "deathless sermon," which aroused his generation to missionary activity, is without parallel since the conversion of Constantine in A.D. 313. Scores of organizations came into being, channeling hundreds of missionaries from Britain, the European continent, and North America to the mission fields of Asia, Africa, and Latin America. The Student Volunteer Movement, founded in 1888, adopted as its motto, "The Evangelization of the World in our Generation," and for a time it seemed as if the goal might be reached. The number of Protestant and Evangelical missionaries in overseas service soon reached 30,000. World War I from 1914 to 1918 brought temporary setbacks, to be followed by an even greater burst of enthusiastic outreach in the 1920s and early 30s. In some respects, the world growth of Christianity reached its high point about 1938. World War II, from 1939 to 1945, caused disruption. The spread of Communism, the increase of secularism, and the "population explosion" in the non-Christian areas of the world slowed the rate of Christian growth to an alarming extent.

A statistical survey published by the International Missionary Council in 1938 estimated the total number of Christians in the world at 718,000,000, as compared with a world population of 2,095,000,000. This meant that about 35 percent of the world was nominally Christian: 18 percent Roman Catholic, 7 percent Orthodox, and 10 percent Protestant and Evangelical. This may have been an optimistic estimate. In any event, the percentages in all Christian categories have declined during the last forty years, not so much because of the lowered growth rate among the churches, as because of the rapid increase of population in regions which are dominantly non-Christian.

World population passed the 3 billion mark in 1960, and then reached 4 billion by 1977. While the total number of Christians had grown to 954 million, as compared to 174 million in Carey's day, this constituted only about 24 percent of the world's people, essentially the same as in 1792. The spectacular growth which was largely the result of the missionary movement of the nineteenth century peaked at 1938, and then was offset by the equally spectacular increase of population, especially in the so-called "Third World," which happened to be the major mission fields of Asia, Africa, and Latin America.

The Achievement

But there is one thing that changing statistics cannot erase! Christianity has been planted in every area of the world, largely as the result of the upsurge of interest and the accelerated activity of the era of William Carey! No longer is the church confined to Western Europe and North America, with only a sprinkling to be found in the rest of the world. Christianity has at last become worldwide in its extent! At least *some* from every major geographical area claim the name of Jesus Christ, and call themselves his disciples.

In Asia, Christians now number over 87 million, with strong indigenous churches seeking to win their fellow countrymen. On the African continent, almost totally unevangelized in Carey's day, Christians now number more than 100 million, and are growing at a rate far higher than the basic population growth. South America claims 166 million Christians, largely Catholic, but with a dynamic Evangelical minority. Oceania (the island world of the Pacific, along with Australia and New Zealand) is more thoroughly evangelized than any comparable territory, with 17 million listed as Christian out of a total population of about 21 million, over 13 million of these being Protestant and Evangelical.

The distinction between "Christian lands" and "non-Christian lands," never accurate, has now almost disappeared, as secularism and paganism are clearly discernible in Europe and North America, and vibrant Christian minorities can be found in nearly every nation. The field has truly become the whole world, with wheat and tares growing side by side in all parts of the ripening harvest. But the presence of churches in the so-called "mission fields" does not mark the end of "foreign missions." The need for the stronger churches of the West to continue strengthening the newly-emerging churches of Asia, Africa, and Latin America is obvious. But the task has become a cooperative effort, as missionaries labor side by side with national pastors, dedicated laymen, and devoted women in many nations of the world. Together they seek to strengthen the growing churches and reach out to the untouched masses. Still a small minority surrounded by overwhelming odds, and opportunities beyond their own potential, the Christians of Asia, Africa, and Latin America call for the assistance and encouragement of their brothers and sisters from the better established and more affluent sections of the World Church.

The task of evangelizing a world of 4 billion, broken into more than 3,000 different tribes and languages, is staggering to contemplate. But the resources available to the church militant were never before so abundant. Modern means of transportation make the remotest areas accessible. New methods of communication multiply the possibilities of reaching the masses, as radio, television, the printed page, cassettes, and other electronic devices are pressed into service for the Lord.

Of course, there are some closed doors. Nearly half the world's population is beyond the reach of regular missionary activity. No foreign missionaries are permitted in the People's Republic of China or the Union of Soviet Socialist Republics. These have a combined population of well over a billion, for whom Christians can only pray and hope that radio programs and printed materials may penetrate where personal witnesses are not able to go. Another half-billion persons are in dominantly Muslim lands where open evangelism is prohibited by law.

Special attention needs to be given to ways of presenting the gospel to Muslims, as increased travel and new methods of communication give some hope of the removal of historic barriers in these lands.

Much of the rest of the world is open and readily accessible. Aside from the Muslim North, most of Africa is open and responsive to the gospel, in spite of the growing threat of Communist influence. Indonesia, the Philippines, and Korea have recently experienced revival and a ripe harvest makes discreet assistance from abroad desirable. Evangelical churches are growing at a record rate in Brazil, and much of Latin America is responsive and welcomes assistance in witnessing in the midst of social revolution.

The religious conditions of the world should constitute, not a deterrent, but a challenge to renewed effort on the part of all true believers. There is evidence that a growing number of Christians are concerned to make it possible for every person on earth to hear the gospel

and have an opportunity either to accept or to reject
the claims of Jesus Christ before the end of the twentieth
century. For those who accept the Bible as the inspired
Word of God, and seek seriously to follow its teaching,
there is no viable alternative. The Scriptures clearly teach
that God does not wish that any should perish, but that
all should come to repentance (2 Pet. 3:9). To his Messiah,
and through him and his followers, God said: "Ask of
Me and I will give you the nations as your inheritance,
the uttermost parts of the earth as your possession" (Ps.
2:8, author's translation). And after giving his life as a
ransom for many, the risen Lord laid the responsibility
upon his followers in all generations in these imperious
words:

Thus it is written, that the [Messiah] should suffer and rise
again from the dead the third day; and that repentance for
forgiveness of sins should be proclaimed in His name to all
the nations, beginning from Jerusalem. You are witnesses of
these things (Luke 24:46-48).

As the Father has sent Me, I also send you. . . . If you
forgive the sins of any, their sins have been forgiven them;
if you retain the sins of any, they have been retained (John
20:21,23).

Go into all the world and preach the gospel to all creation
(Mark 16:15).

All authority has been given to Me in heaven and on earth.
Go therefore and make disciples of all the nations, baptizing
them in the name of the Father and the Son and the Holy
Spirit, teaching them to observe all that I commanded you;
and lo, I am with you always, even to the end of the age
(Matt. 28:18-20).

But you shall receive power when the Holy Spirit has come
upon you; and you shall be My witnesses both in Jerusalem,
and in all Judea and Samaria, and even to the remotest part
of the earth (Acts 1:8).

Notes

[1] The usual definition of a tribe is "a cluster or group of people sharing a common name, language, culture, and territory." See R. Pierce Beaver, *The Gospel and Frontier Peoples*, p. 240.

[2] In 1959 the story of Wycliffe Bible Translators was published under the title, *Two Thousand Tongues to Go,* because of a statement by the founder, W. Cameron Townsend, indicating the remaining task of Bible translation. Bible Society experts now refer to 5,000 language groups, although some are so small that no translation may be attempted.

[3] See *The Gospel and Frontier Peoples,* edited by R. Pierce Beaver, William Carey Library, 1973, pp. 233-310.

[4] *Ibid.,* pp. 242 ff., 305.

[5] Kenneth Scott Latourette, *A History of the Expansion of Christianity,* Volume II. Harper, New York, 1938.

[6] *Carey's Enquiry,* a facsimile reprint, 1942, Baptist Missionary Society, 19 Furnival Street, London, E. C. 4, p. 62.

[7] *Op. cit.,* p. 67.

[8] *Ibid.,* p. 7.

[9] *Ibid.,* p. 8.

[10] *Ibid.,* p. 9.

RELIGIOUS POPULATION OF THE WORLD

Total Christians	951,058,100
Roman Catholic	542,521,000
Eastern Orthodox	84,803,200
Protestant and Evangelical	323,724,500
Jewish	14,532,895
Muslim	537,713,400
Zoroastrian	228,480
Shinto	61,156,000
Taoist	29,284,100
Confucian	175,688,850
Buddhist	244,800,300
Hindu	518,794,150
Sikh	12,000,000
Total Adherents of World Religions	2,545,256,275
TOTAL WORLD POPULATION	4,044,433,000
Unaffiliated with Any Known Faith	1,499,176,725

Statistics from *The World Almanac and Book of Facts, 1978.* Newspaper Enterprises Association, Inc., New York, 1977, p. 348.